Contemporary Broadway

Contents

ISBN 0-634-00066-7

HAL•LEONARD®
CORPORATION

7777 W. BLUEMOUND RD. P.O. BOX 13819 MILWAUKEE, WI 53213

Visit Hal Leonard Online at
www.halleonard.com

ALONE AT THE DRIVE-IN MOVIE

from GREASE

Lyric and Music by WARREN CASEY
and JIM JACOBS

3

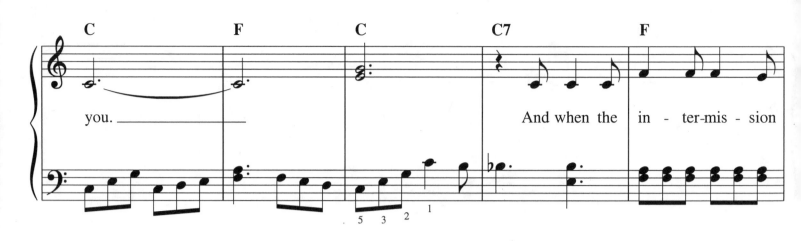

AND ALL THAT JAZZ
from CHICAGO

Words by FRED EBB
Music by JOHN KANDER

Brightly

1. Come on, babe, _ why don't we paint the town, _
2. Slick your hair _ and wear your buck - le shoes _
3. *(See additional lyrics)*

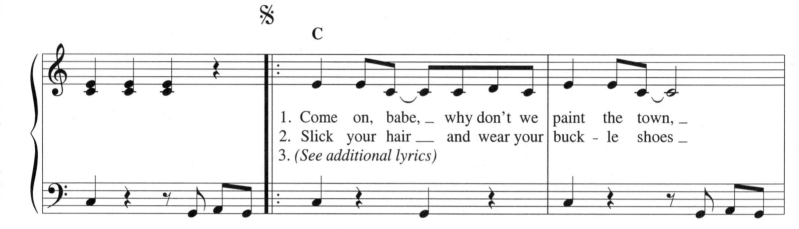

and all that jazz! _ I'm gon - na rouge my knees _ and roll my
and all that jazz! _ I hear that Fa - ther Dip _ is gon - na

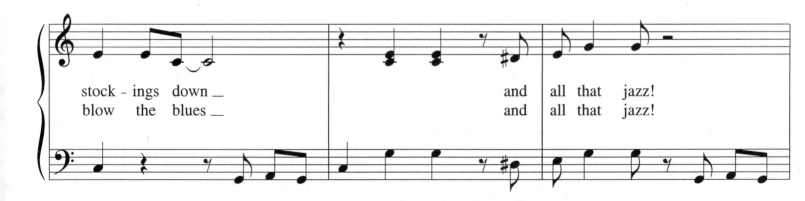

stock - ings down _ and all that jazz!
blow the blues _ and all that jazz!

Additional Lyrics

3. Find a flask, we're playing fast and loose
   And all that jazz!
   Right up here is where I store the juice
   And all that jazz!

   Come on, babe, we're gonna brush the sky.
   I betcha Lucky Lindy never flew so high,
   'Cause in the stratosphere how could he lend an ear to
   All that jazz!

AS IF WE NEVER SAID GOODBYE

from SUNSET BOULEVARD

Music by ANDREW LLOYD WEBBER
Lyrics by DON BLACK and CHRISTOPHER HAMPTON,
with contributions by AMY POWERS

Slowly

Norma: I don't know why I'm fright - ened I

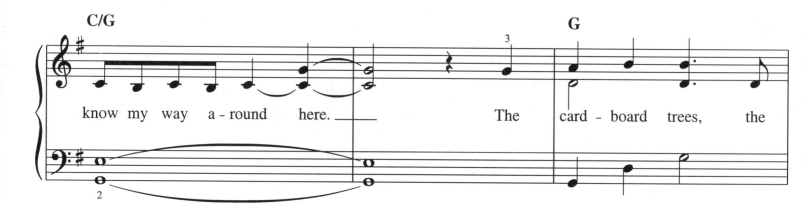

know my way a - round here. The card - board trees, the

paint - ed seas, the sound here. Yes, a

world to re - dis - cov - er, but I'm not in an - y hur - ry,

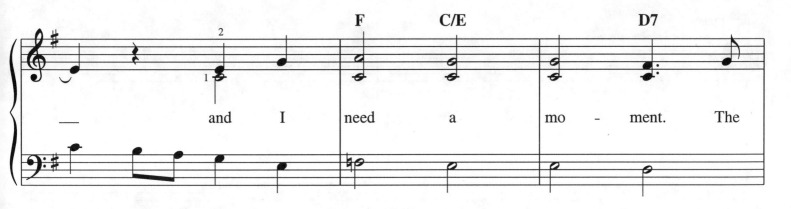

and I need a mo - ment. The

whis - pered con - ver - sa - tions _____ in

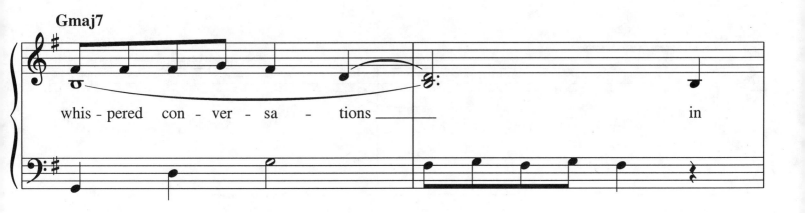

ov - er-crowd-ed hall - ways, _____ the at - mos - phere_ as

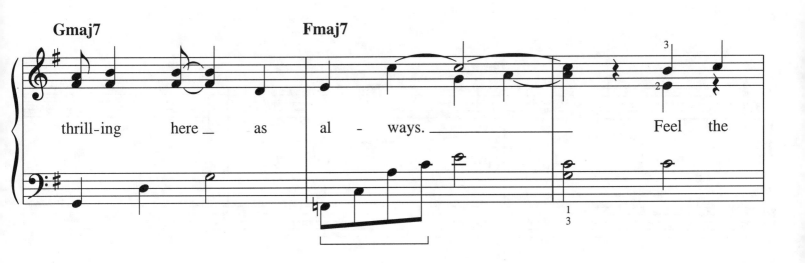

thrill-ing here _ as al - ways. _____ Feel the

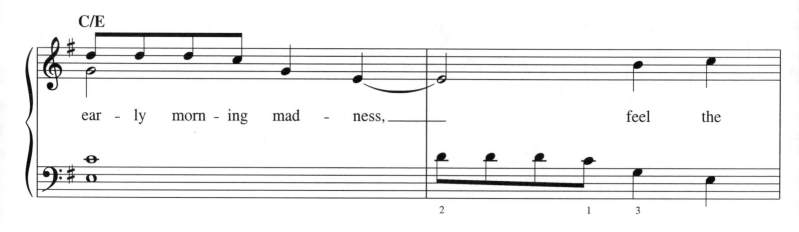

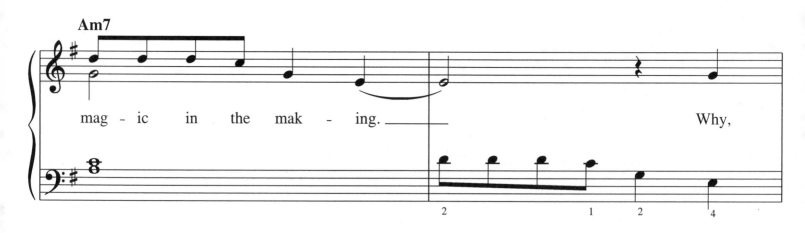

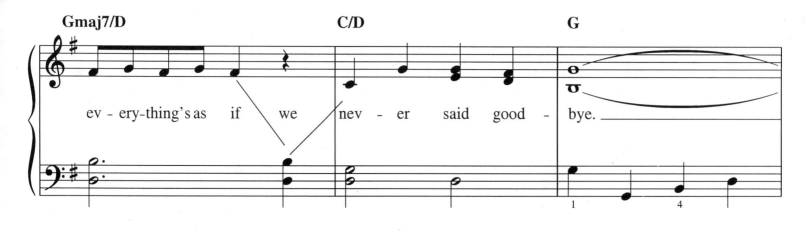

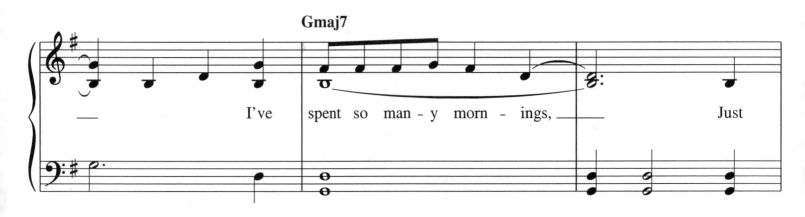

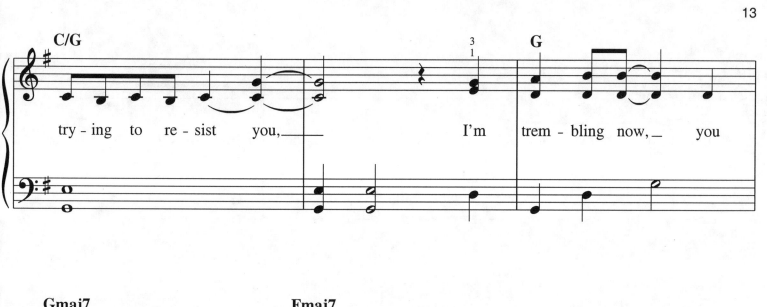

try - ing to re - sist you, ___ I'm trem - bling now, __ you

can't know how _ I've missed you, _____ missed the

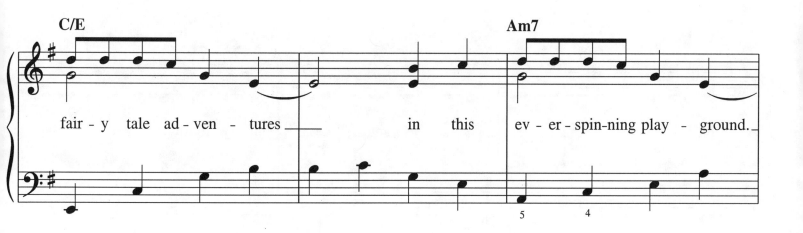

fair - y tale ad - ven - tures ___ in this ev - er - spin-ning play - ground. _

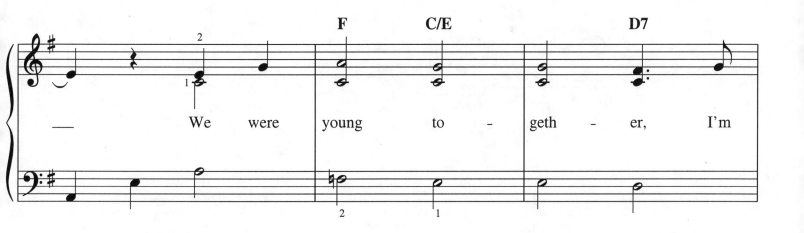

_ We were young to - geth - er, I'm

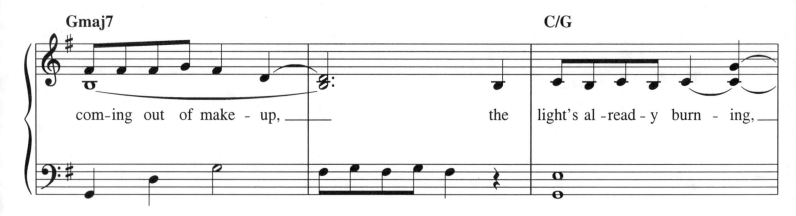

com-ing out of make - up, _____ the light's al -read -y burn - ing, _____

_____ not long un - til ___ the cam - eras will _ start

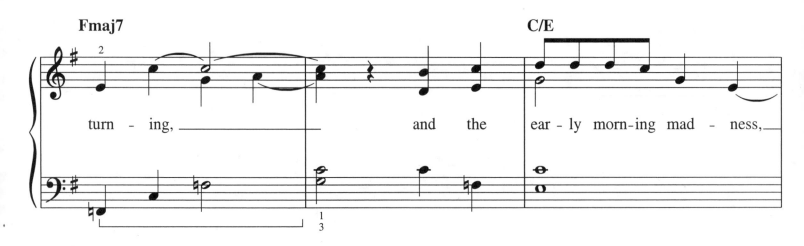

turn - ing, _____ and the ear - ly morn-ing mad - ness,

_____ and the mag-ic in the mak - ing, _____ yes,

ev - ery-thing's as if we nev - er said good - bye.

I don't want to be a - lone, that's all in the

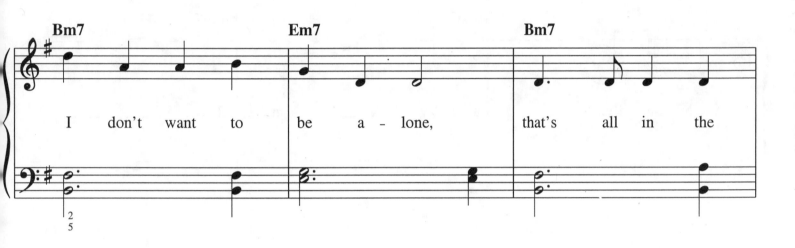

past. This world's wait - ed long e - nough,

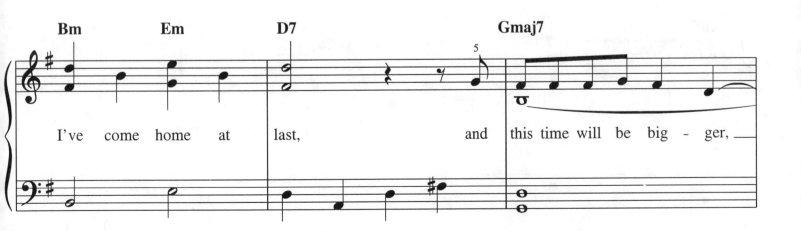

I've come home at last, and this time will be big - ger,

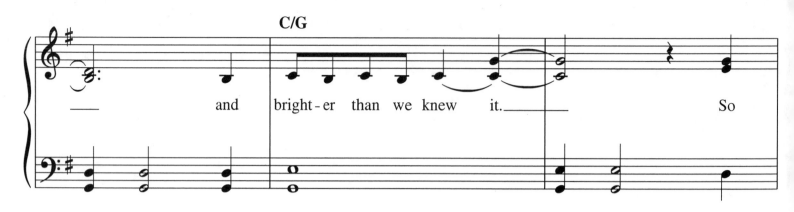

and bright-er than we knew it.___ So

watch me fly,___ we all know I___ can do it.___

Could I stop my hand from shak - ing?___ Has there

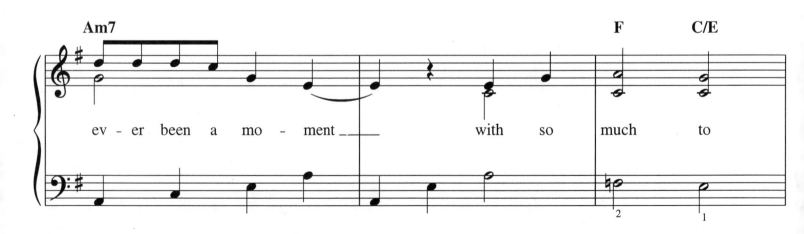

ev - er been a mo - ment ___ with so much to

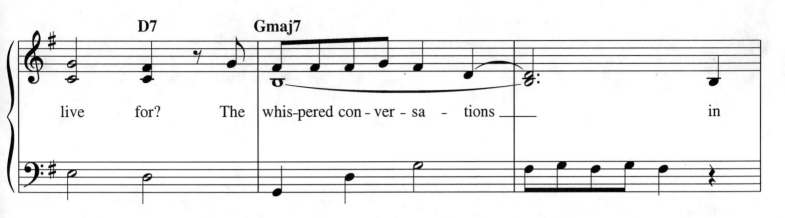

live for? The whis-pered con - ver - sa - tions _____ in

ov - er-crowd-ed hall - ways, _____ so much to say, _____ not

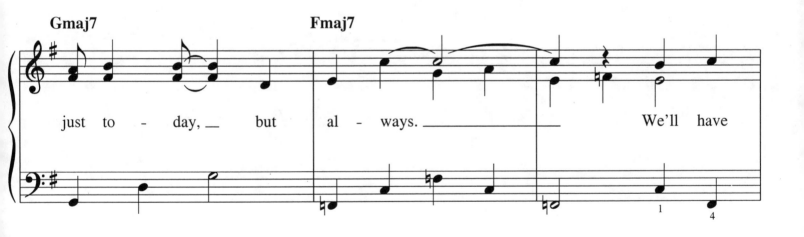

just to - day, _____ but al - ways. _____ We'll have

ear - ly morn-ing mad - ness, _____ we'll have mag - ic in the mak - ing, _____

yes, ev - ery-thing's as if we nev - er said good -

bye, yes, ev-ery-thing's as if we

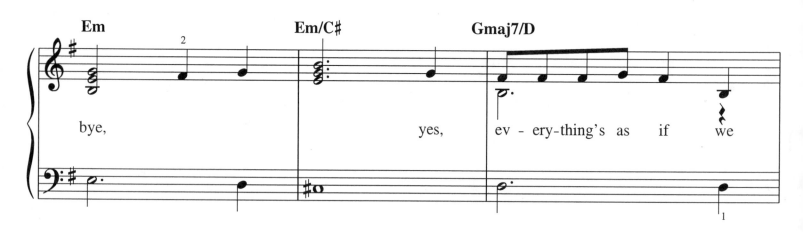

nev - er said good - bye. We taught the

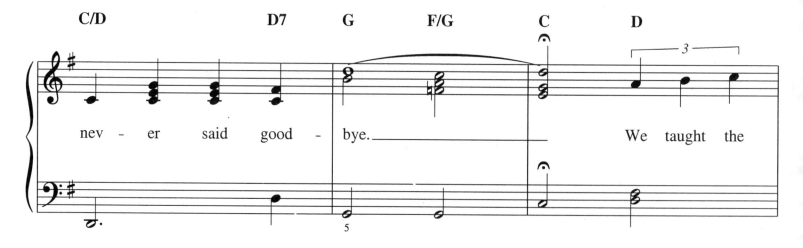

world new ways to dream.

rit.

BEAUTY AND THE BEAST
from Walt Disney's BEAUTY AND THE BEAST: THE BROADWAY MUSICAL

Lyrics by HOWARD ASHMAN
Music by ALAN MENKEN

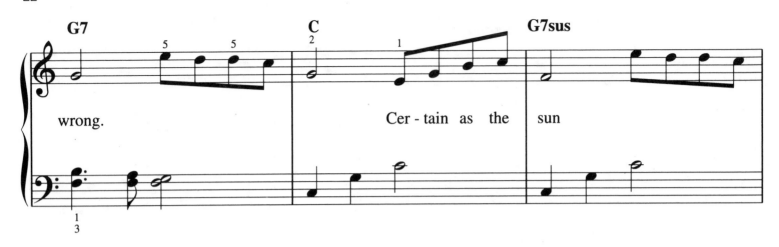

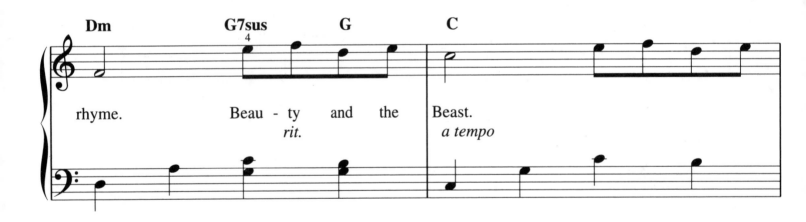

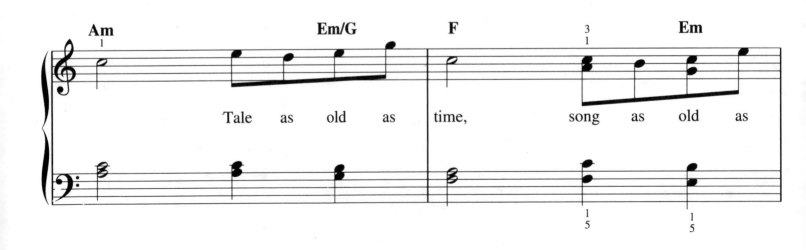

rhyme.   Beau - ty and the   Beast.

a tempo

BE PREPARED

Disney Presents THE LION KING: THE BROADWAY MUSICAL

Music by ELTON JOHN
Lyrics by TIM RICE

Steadily, rhythmically

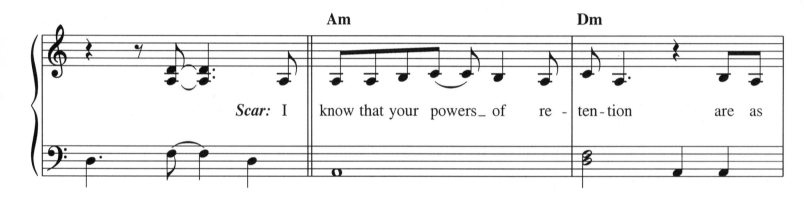

Scar: I know that your powers of re-ten-tion are as

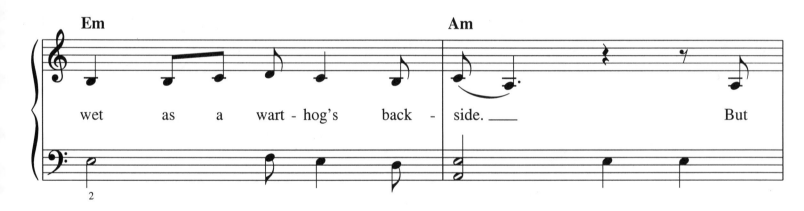

wet as a wart-hog's back-side. ___ But

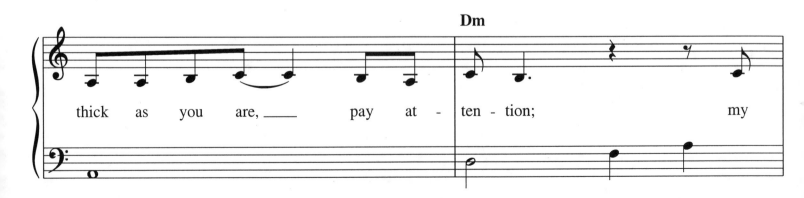

thick as you are, ___ pay at-ten-tion; my

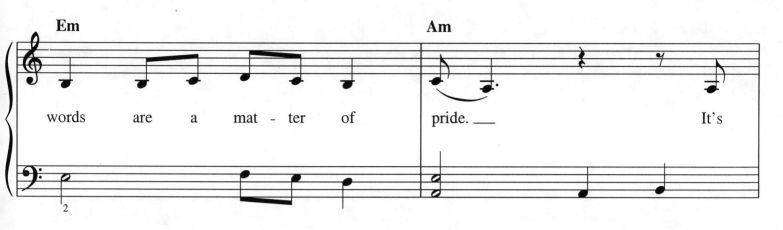

words are a mat - ter of pride. ___ It's

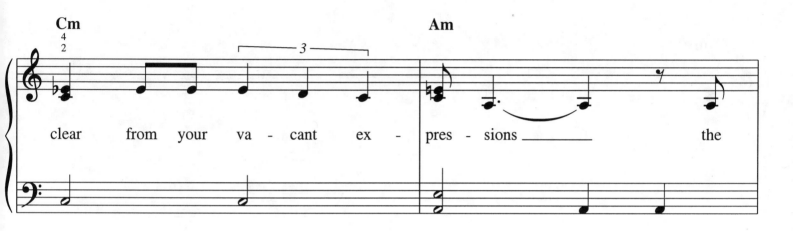

clear from your va - cant ex - pres - sions ___ the

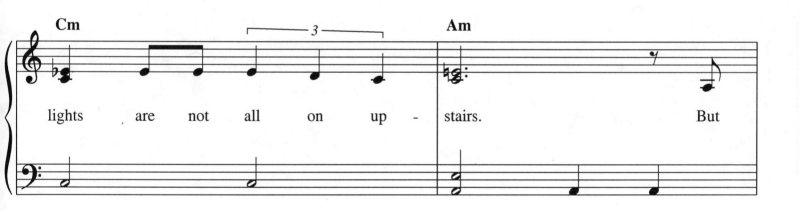

lights are not all on up - stairs. But

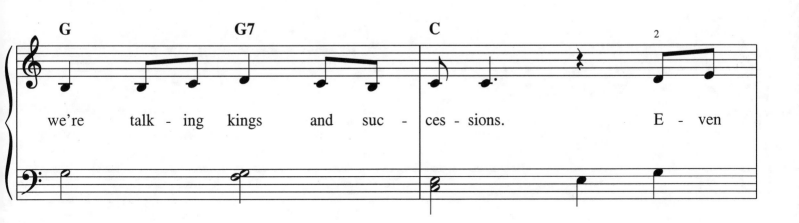

we're talk - ing kings and suc - ces - sions. E - ven

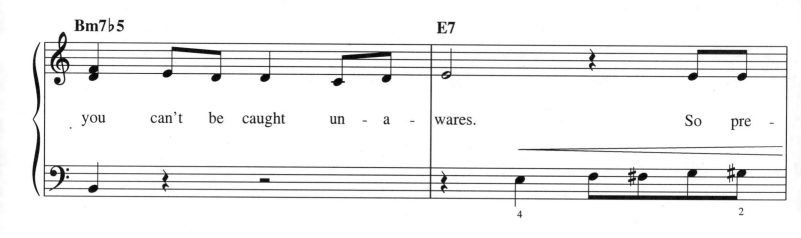

you can't be caught un - a - wares. So pre -

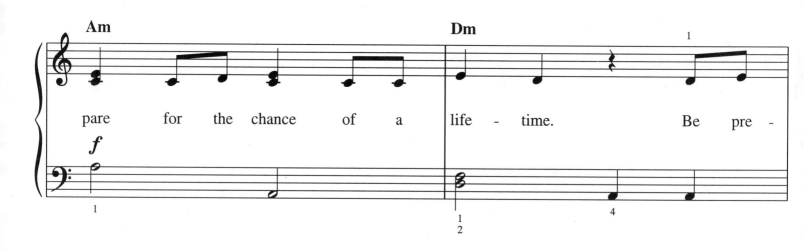

pare for the chance of a life - time. Be pre -

pared for sen - sa - tion - al news. A

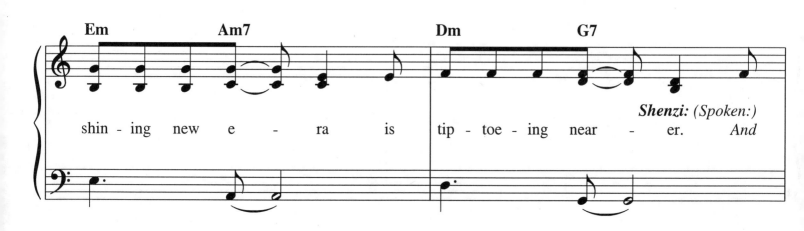

shin - ing new e - ra is tip - toe - ing near - er. *And*

Shenzi: (Spoken:)

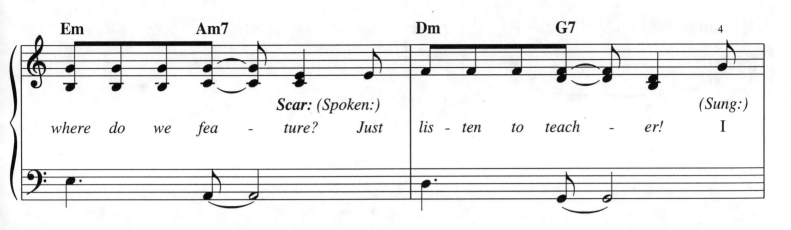

Scar: (Spoken:) *where do we fea - ture? Just* **(Sung:)** *lis - ten to teach - er! I*

know it sounds sor - did, but you'll be re - ward - ed when at

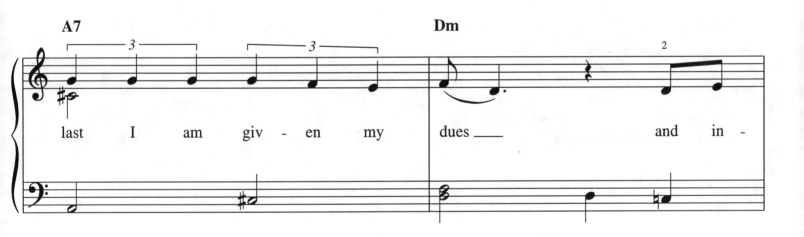

last I am giv - en my dues ___ and in -

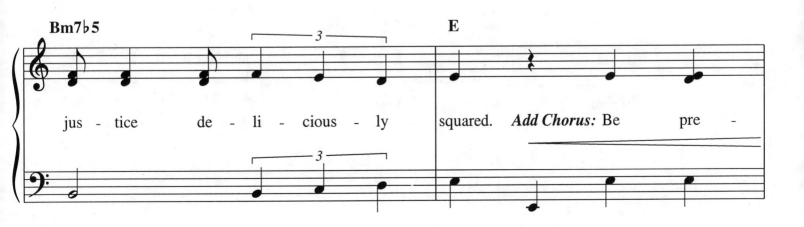

jus - tice de - li - cious - ly squared. ***Add Chorus:*** Be pre -

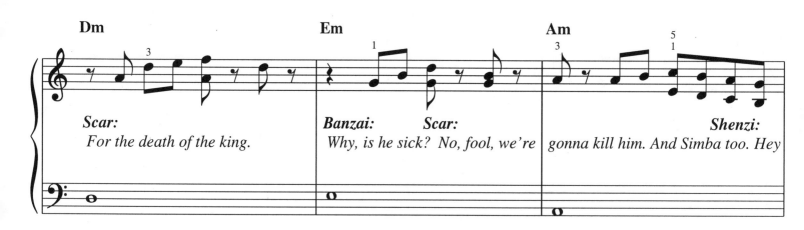

Cm ... **Am** ... **G**

never go hungry again! | *Shenzi:* Yay! | *Banzai:* Yeah, alright! | Shenzi: Alright!

C ... **Bm7♭5** ... **E**

Long live the King! | *Other Hyenas:* Long live the King! Ha ha ha! | *Chorus:* It's

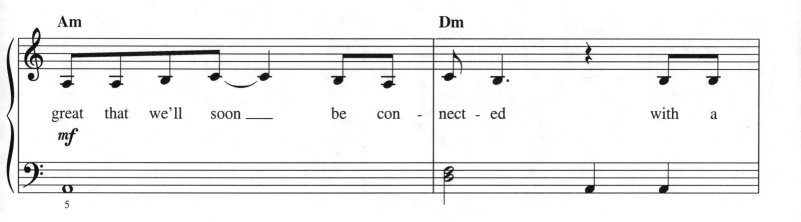

Am ... **Dm**

great that we'll soon ___ be con - nect - ed with a

mf

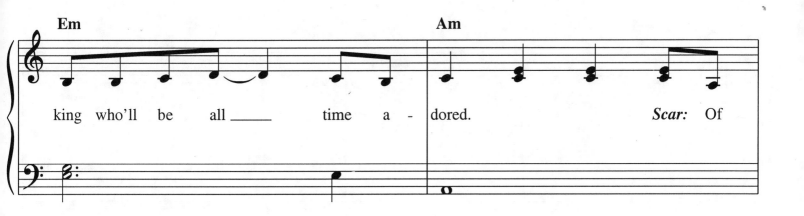

Em ... **Am**

king who'll be all ___ time a - dored. | *Scar:* Of

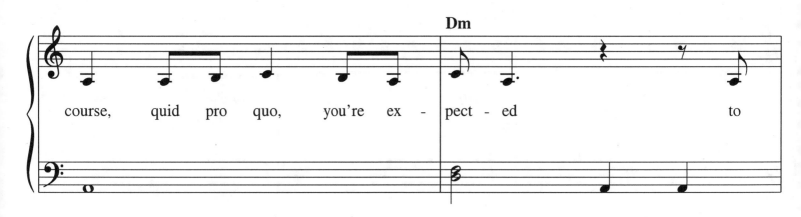

course, quid pro quo, you're ex - pect - ed to

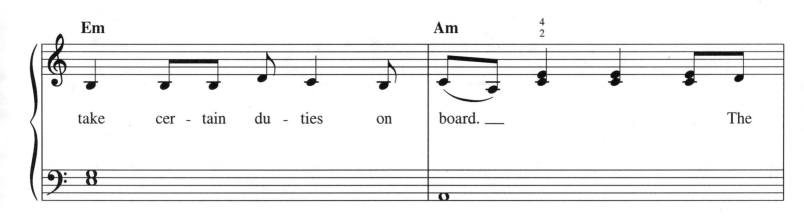

take cer - tain du - ties on board. ___ The

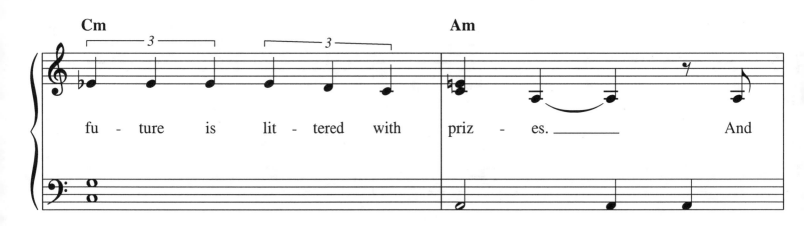

fu - ture is lit - tered with priz - es. _____ And

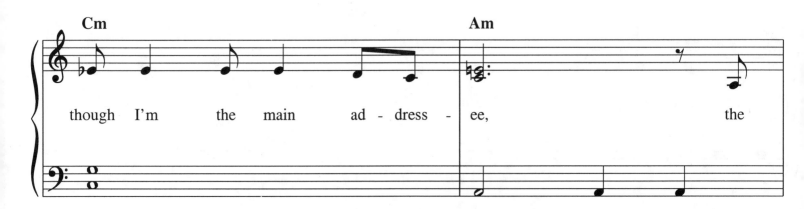

though I'm the main ad - dress - ee, the

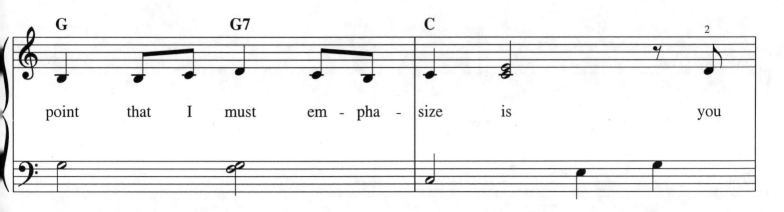

point that I must em - pha - size is you

won't get a sniff with - out me! So pre -

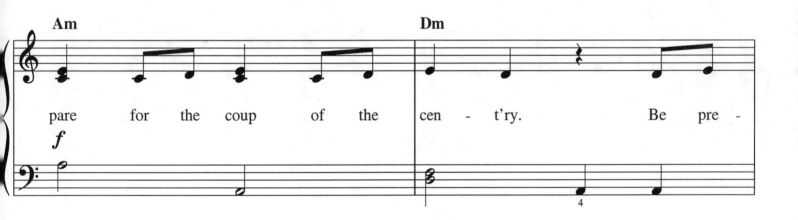

pare for the coup of the cen - t'ry. Be pre -

pared for the murk - i - est scam. Me -

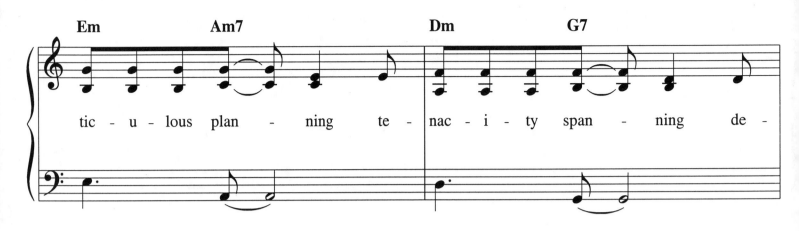

tic - u - lous plan - ning te - nac - i - ty span - ning de -

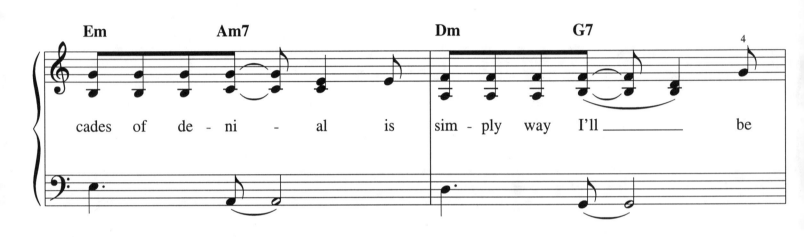

cades of de - ni - al is sim - ply way I'll _____ be

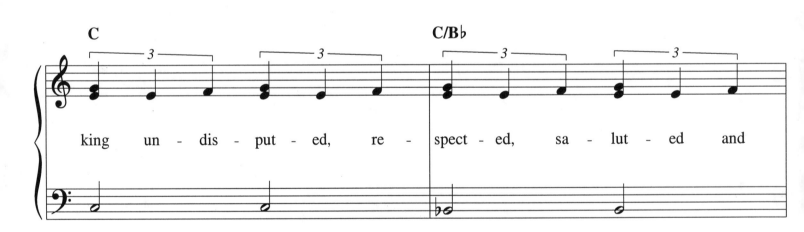

king un - dis - put - ed, re - spect - ed, sa - lut - ed and

seen for the won - der I am. Yes, my

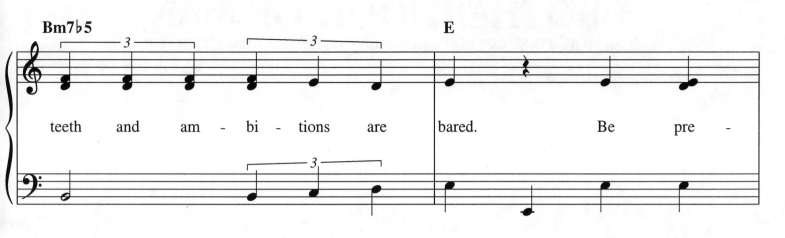

teeth and am - bi - tions are bared. Be pre -

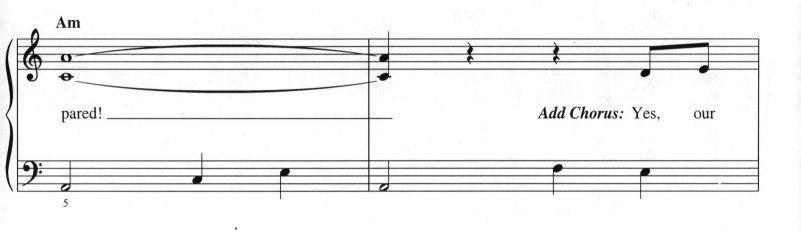

pared! _____ *Add Chorus:* Yes, our

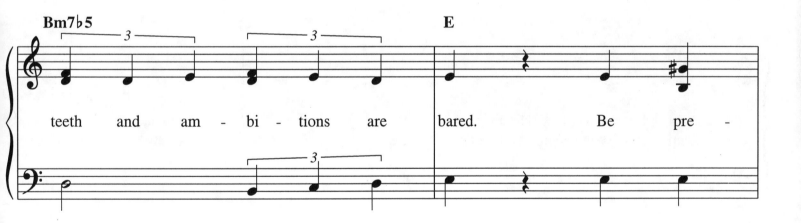

teeth and am - bi - tions are bared. Be pre -

pared!

Wild laughter
molto rit.

BROTHERHOOD OF MAN

from HOW TO SUCCEED IN BUSINESS WITHOUT REALLY TRYING

By FRANK LOESSER

CABARET
from the Musical CABARET

Words by FRED EBB
Music by JOHN KANDER

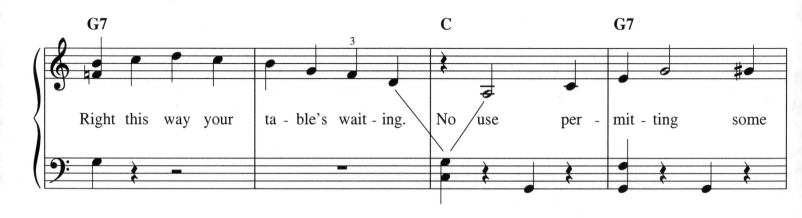

Right this way your ta - ble's wait - ing. No use per - mit - ting some

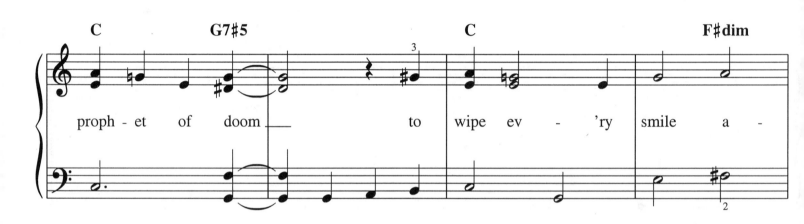

proph - et of doom ___ to wipe ev - 'ry smile a -

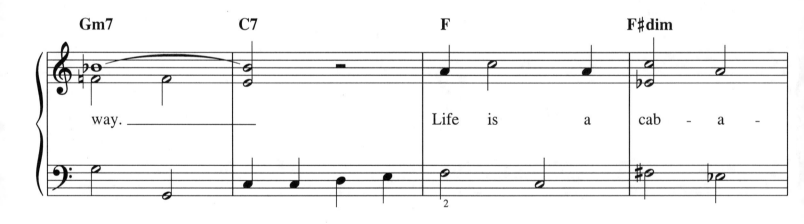

way. ___ Life is a cab - a -

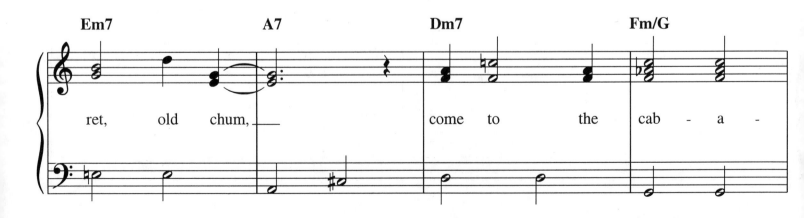

ret, old chum, ___ come to the cab - a -

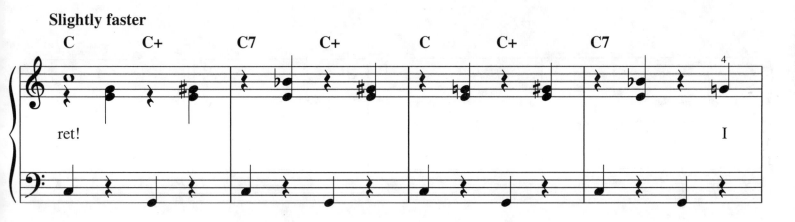

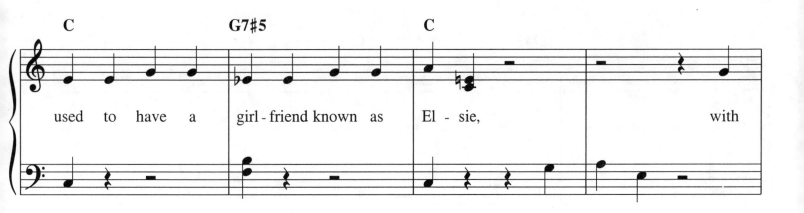

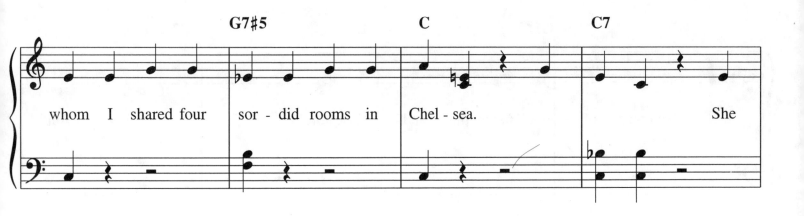

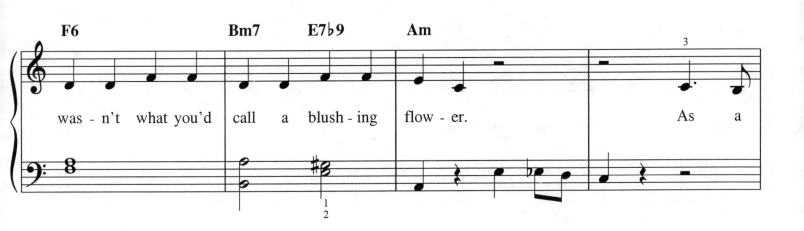

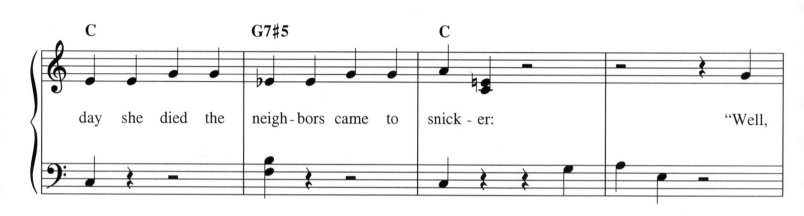

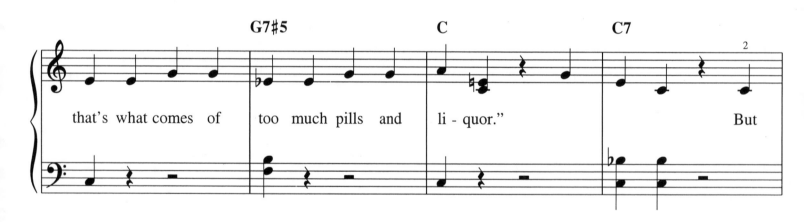

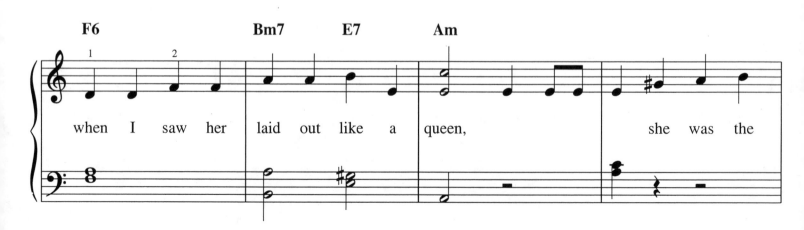

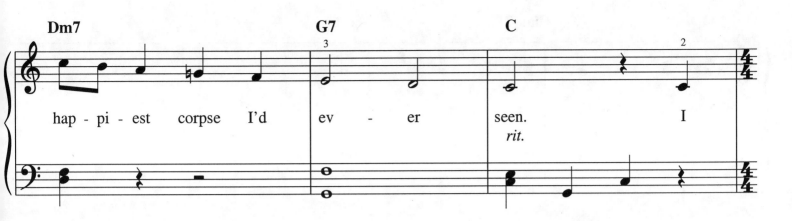

Dm7 | **G7** | **C**

hap - pi - est corpse I'd ev – er seen.
rit.
I

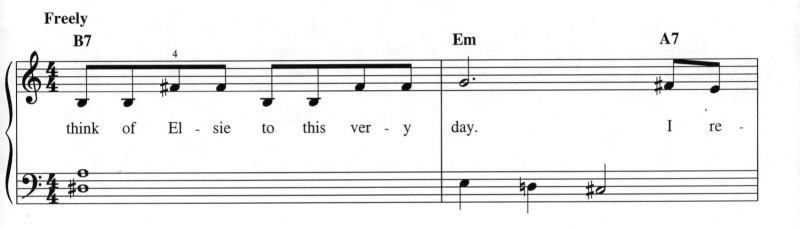

Freely
B7 | **Em** | **A7**

think of El - sie to this ver - y day.
I re -

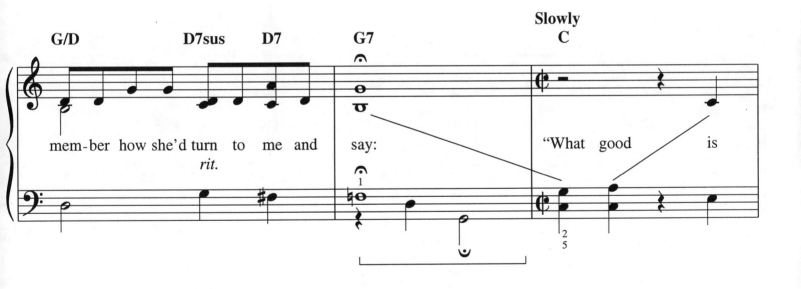

G/D | **D7sus** | **D7** | **G7** | **Slowly** | **C**

mem - ber how she'd turn to me and say:
rit.
"What good is

G7 | **C** | **G7#5**

sit - ting a - lone in your room?

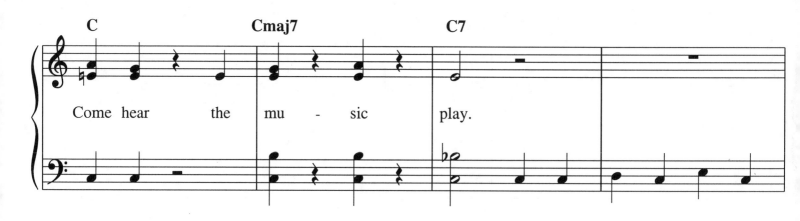

C   **Cmaj7**   **C7**

Come hear   the   mu - sic   play.

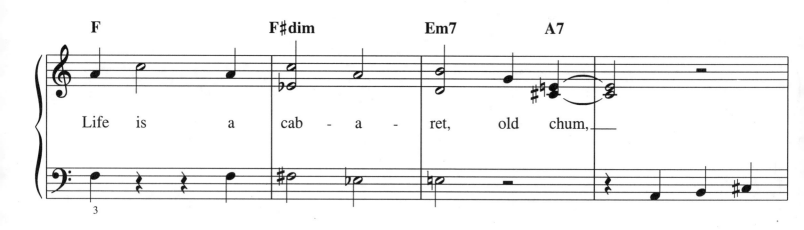

F   **F♯dim**   **Em7**   **A7**

Life   is   a   cab - a - ret,   old chum,___

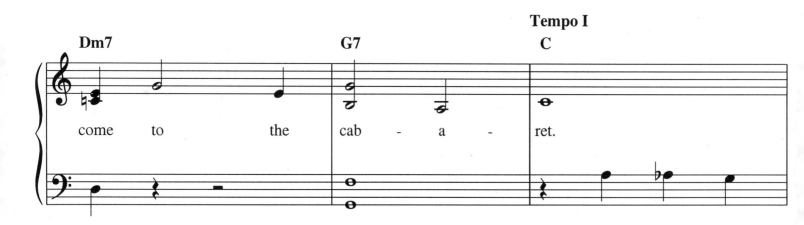

Tempo I

Dm7   **G7**   **C**

come   to   the   cab - a - ret.

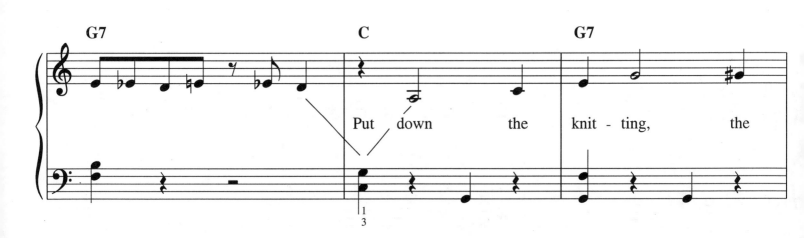

G7   **C**   **G7**

Put down   the   knit - ting,   the

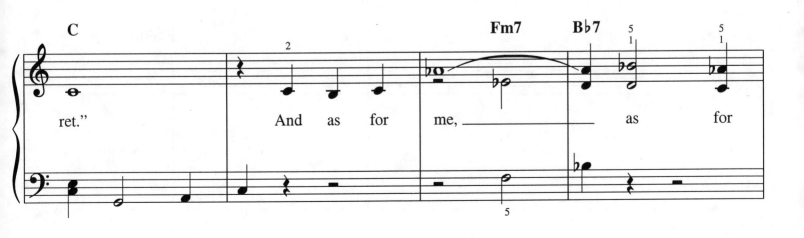

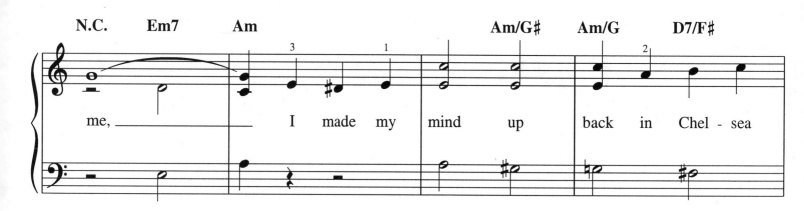

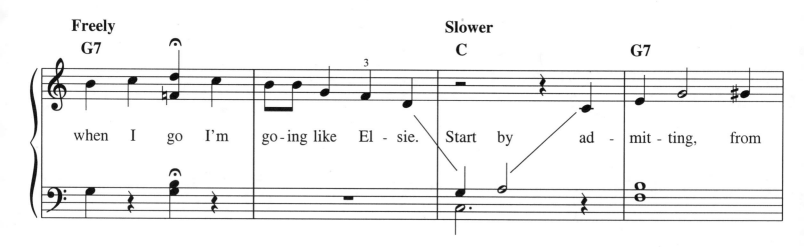

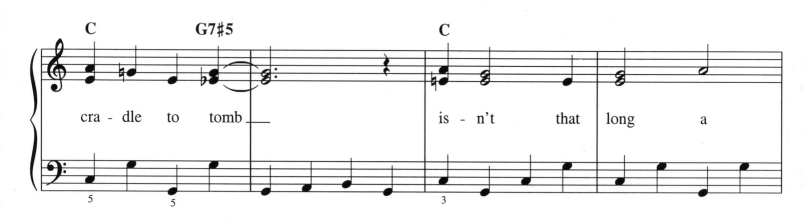

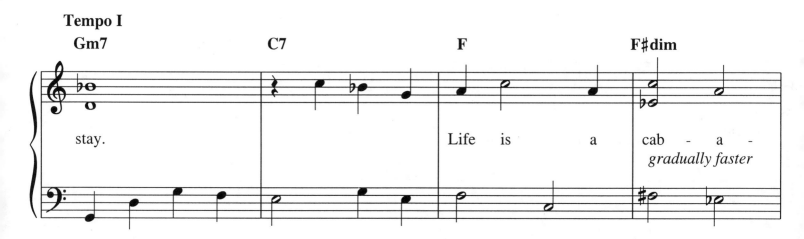

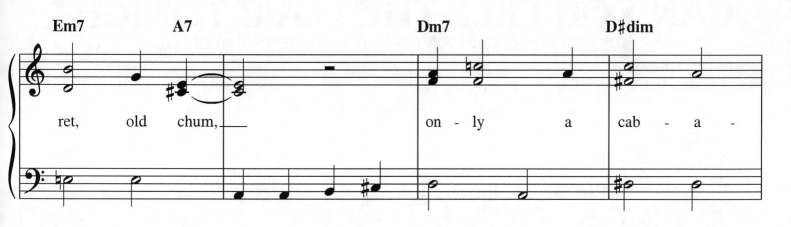

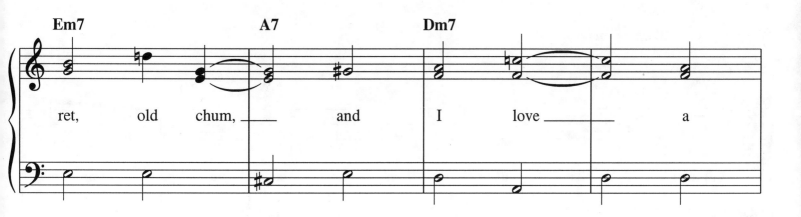

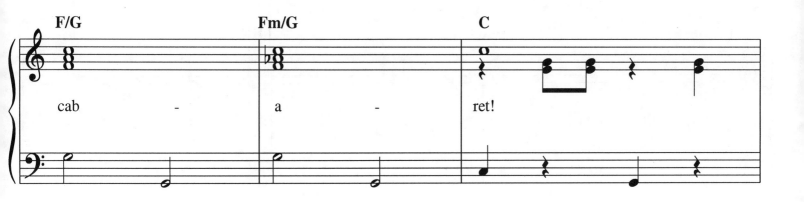

CAN YOU FEEL THE LOVE TONIGHT

Disney Presents THE LION KING: THE BROADWAY MUSICAL

Music by ELTON JOHN
Lyrics by TIM RICE

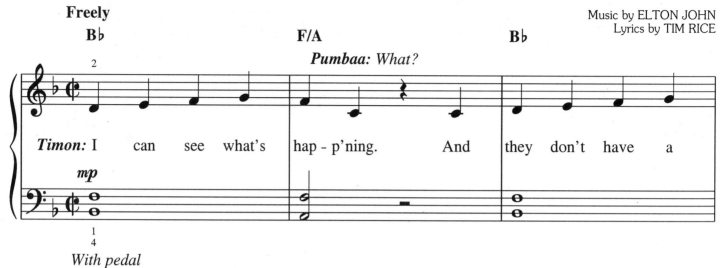

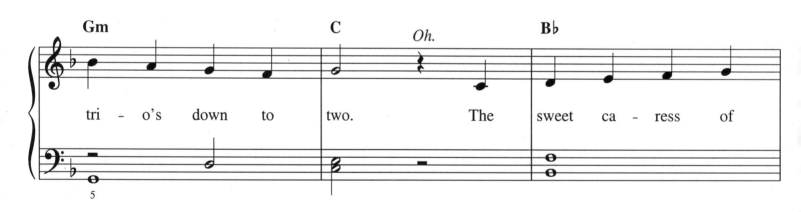

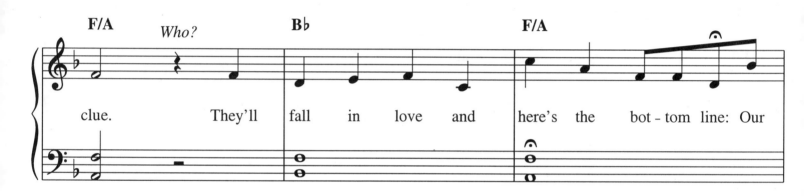

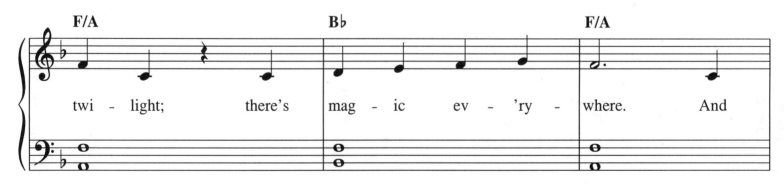

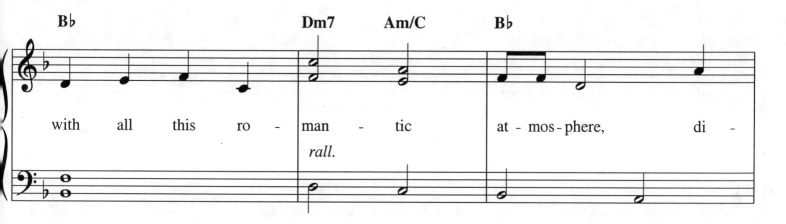

with all this ro - man - tic at - mos - phere, di -
rall.

Moderately (in two)

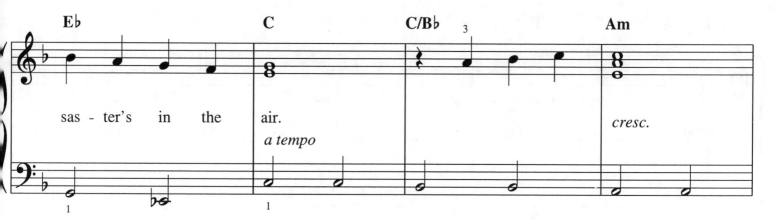

sas - ter's in the air.
a tempo
cresc.

Chorus: Can you feel ___ the love ___
mf

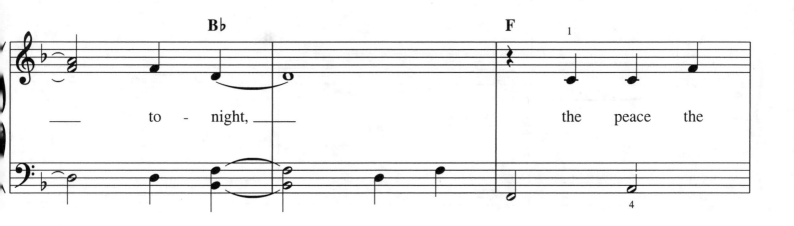

___ to - night, ___ the peace the

48

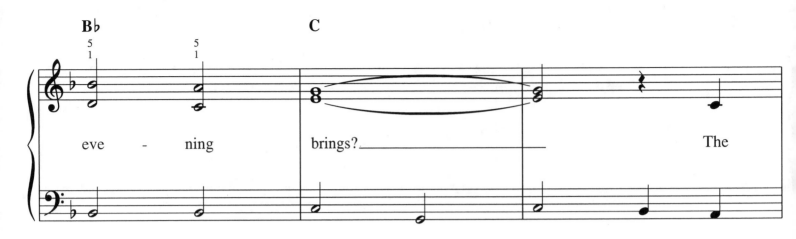

eve - ning   brings?   The

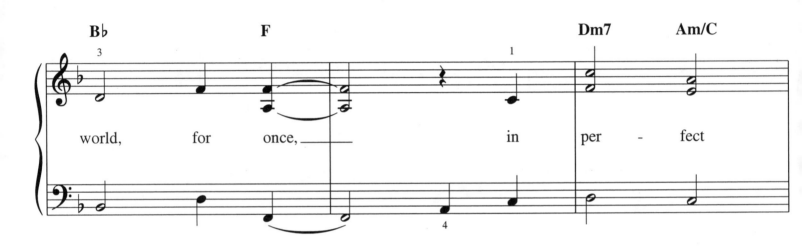

world,   for   once,   in   per - fect

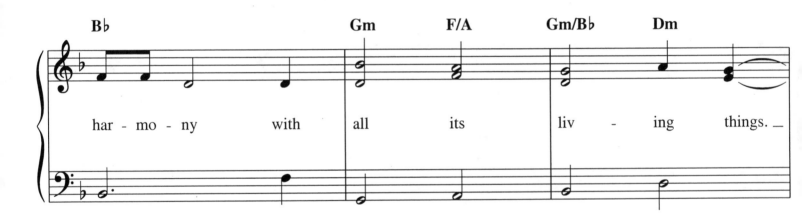

har - mo - ny   with   all   its   liv - ing   things.

dim.

Simba: So   man - y   things   to

mp

tell her,   but   how   to   make   her   see   the

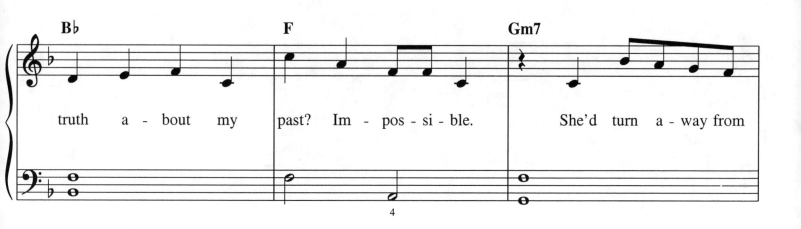

truth   a - bout   my   past? Im - pos - si - ble.   She'd turn a - way from

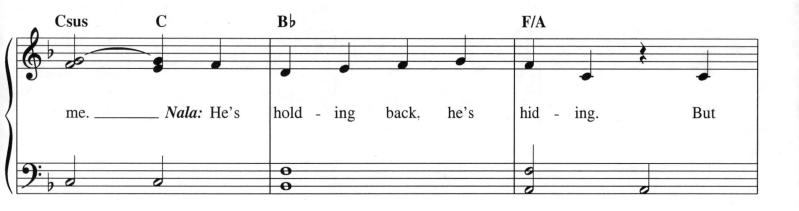

me. _____ *Nala:* He's   hold - ing   back, he's   hid - ing.   But

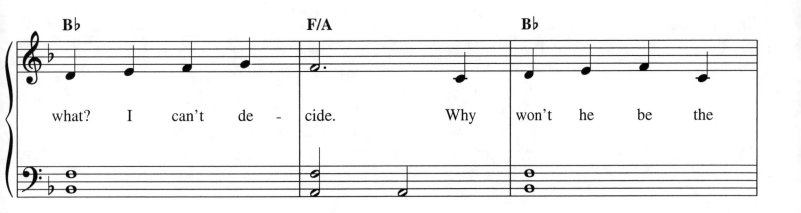

what?   I   can't de -   cide.   Why   won't   he   be   the

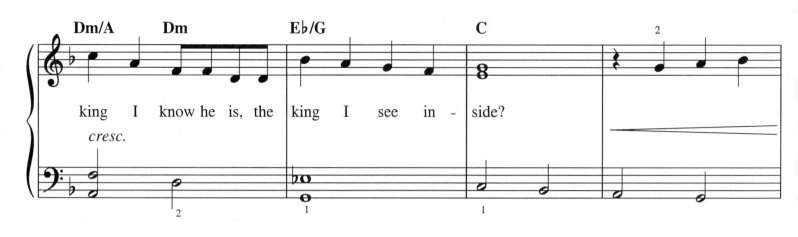

king I know he is, the king I see in - side?

cresc.

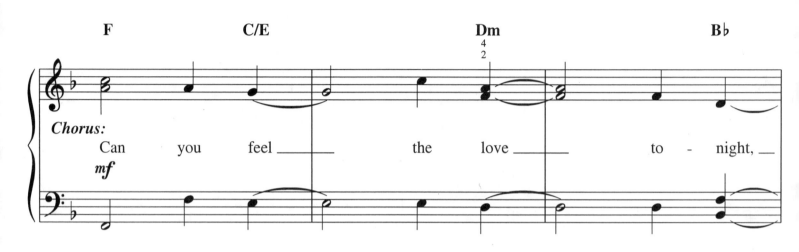

Chorus:

Can you feel the love to - night,

mf

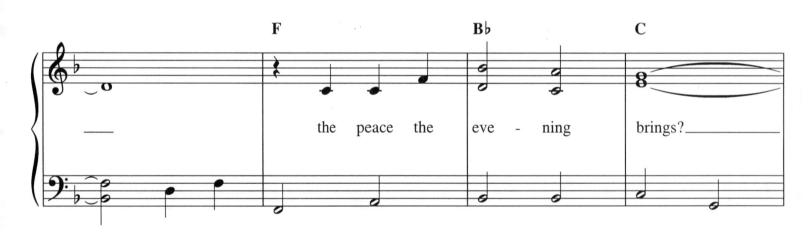

the peace the eve - ning brings?

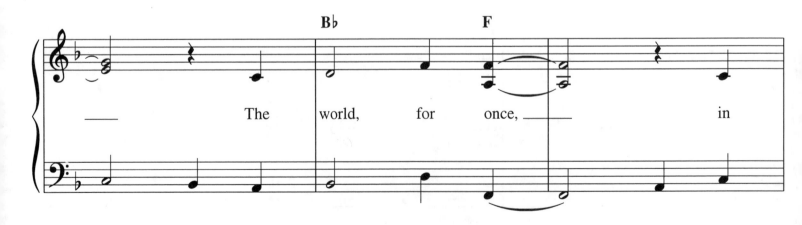

The world, for once, in

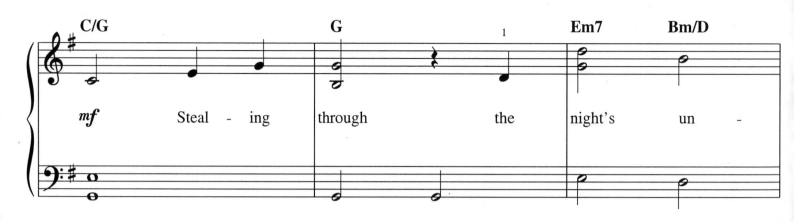

Steal - ing through the night's un -

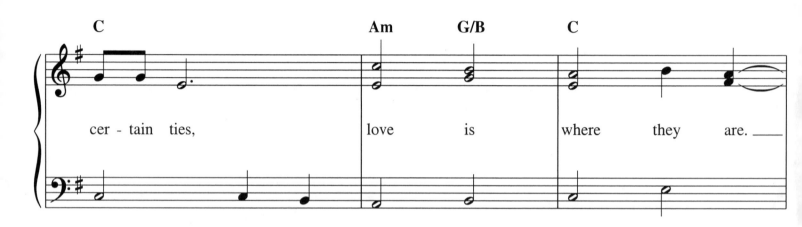

cer - tain ties, love is where they are. ___

___ *Timon:* And if he

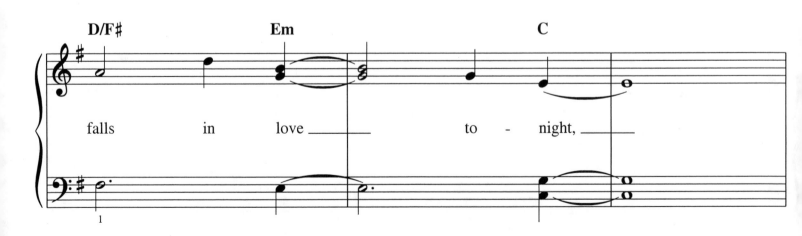

falls in love ___ to - night, ___

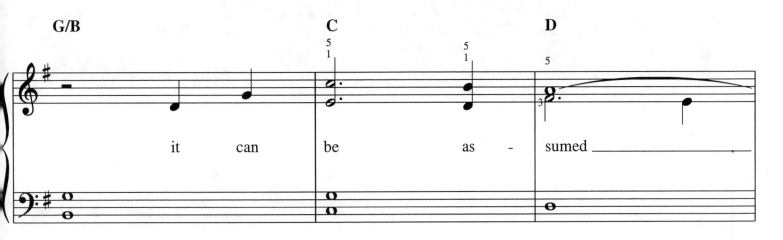

G/B   **C**   **D**

it can be as - sumed

C   **G/B**

Pumbaa: his care - free days with

Em7   **Bm/D**   **C**   **Am**   **G/B**

us are his - tory, in short, our

Timon And Pumbaa:

rall.

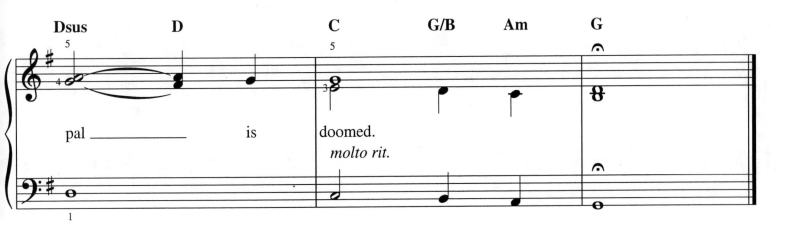

Dsus   **D**   **C**   **G/B**   **Am**   **G**

pal is doomed.

molto rit.

COMEDY TONIGHT
from A FUNNY THING HAPPENED ON THE WAY TO THE FORUM

Words and Music by
STEPHEN SONDHEIM

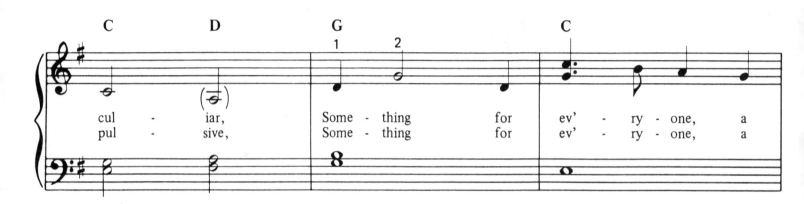

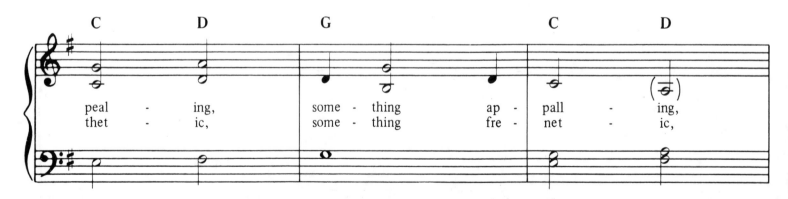

Some - thing for ev' - ry - one, a com - edy to -
Some - thing for ev' - ry - one, a com - edy to -

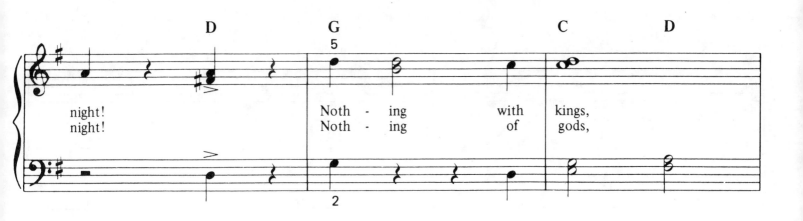

night! Noth - ing with kings,
night! Noth - ing of gods,

Noth - ing with crowns; Bring on the
Noth - ing of fate, Weight - y af -

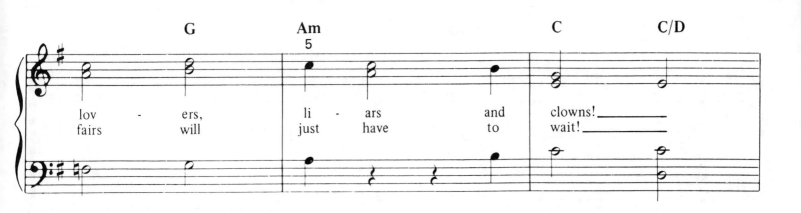

lov - ers, li - ars and clowns!_____
fairs will just have to wait!_____

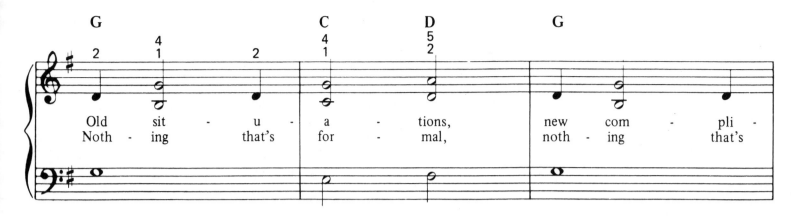

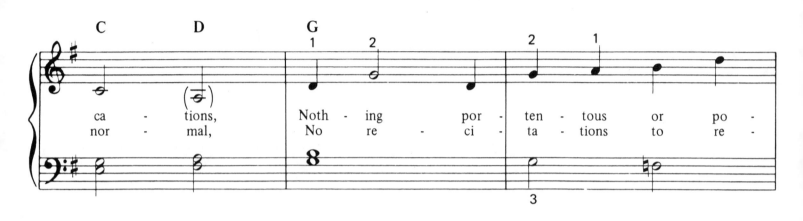

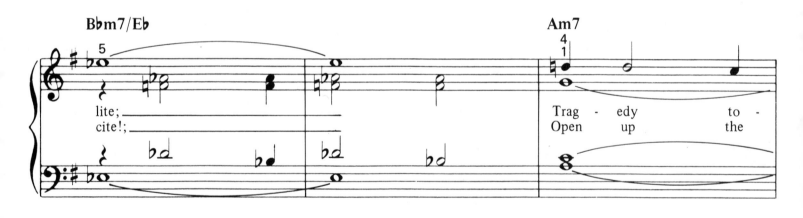

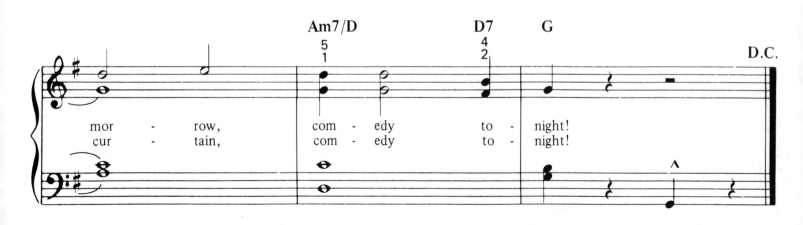

I BELIEVE IN YOU
from HOW TO SUCCEED IN BUSINESS WITHOUT REALLY TRYING

By FRANK LOESSER

Moderate swing feel

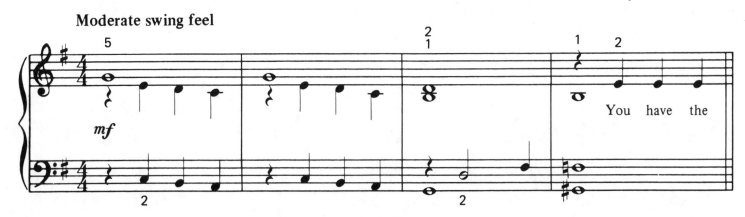

You have the

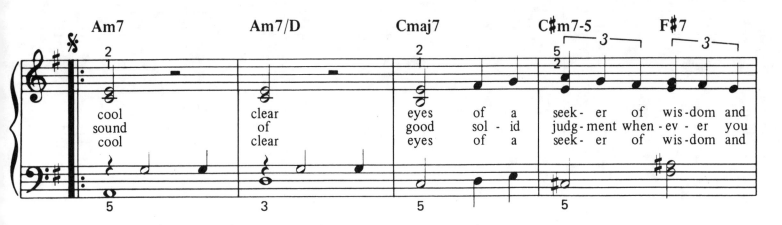

cool clear eyes of a seek-er of wis-dom and
sound of good sol-id judg-ment when-ev-er you
cool clear eyes of a seek-er of wis-dom and

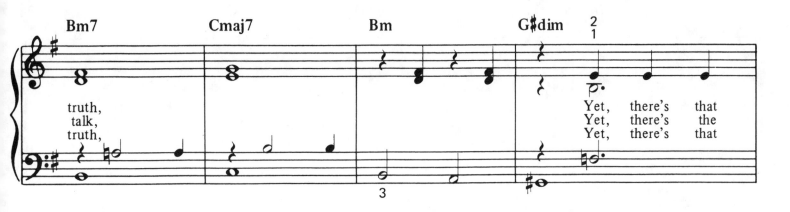

truth, Yet, there's that
talk, Yet, there's the
truth, Yet, there's that

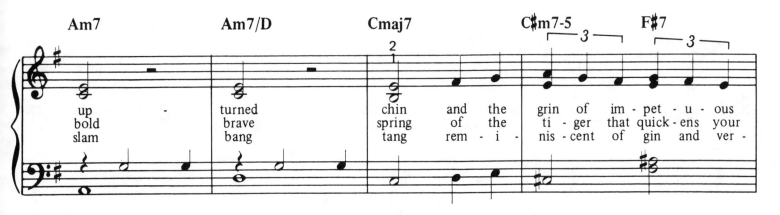

up - turned chin and the grin of im-pet-u-ous
bold brave spring of the ti-ger that quick-ens your
slam bang tang rem-i-nis-cent of gin and ver-

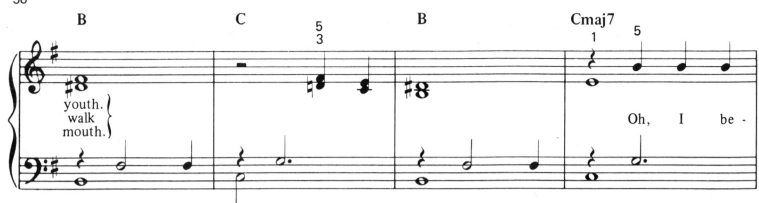

youth.
walk
mouth.

Oh, I be-

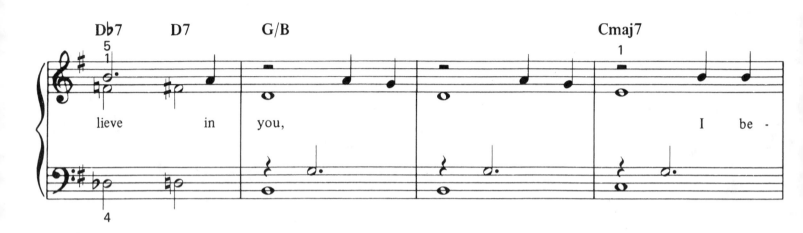

lieve in you, I be-

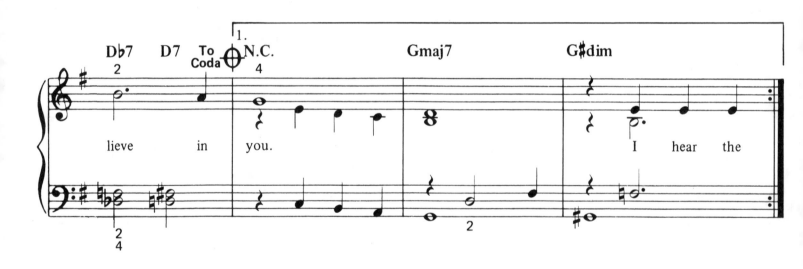

lieve in you. I hear the

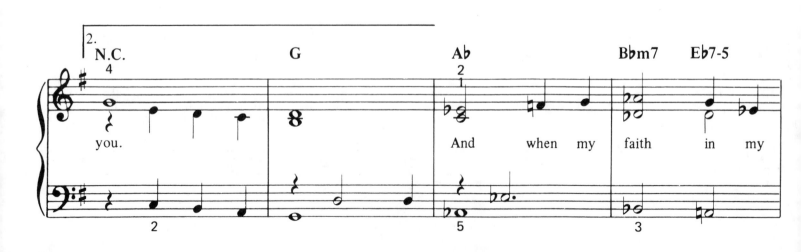

you. And when my faith in my

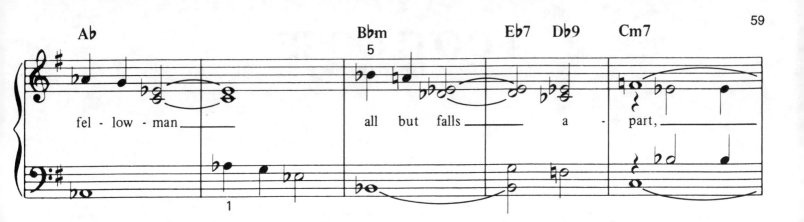

fel - low - man ____ all but falls ____ a - part, ____

____ I've but to feel your hand grasp - ing mine ____

____ and I take heart, ____ I take heart.

to see the   you.

FOOTLOOSE
from FOOTLOOSE

Words by DEAN PITCHFORD and KENNY LOGGINS
Music by KENNY LOGGINS

I been work - in' so hard.
You're play - in' so cool,

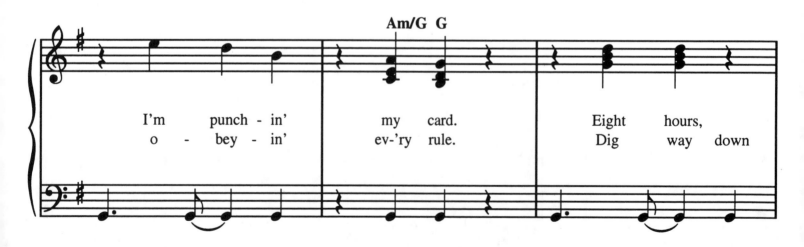

I'm punch - in' my card.
o - bey - in' ev'ry rule.

Eight hours,
Dig way down

GODSPEED TITANIC (SAIL ON)

from TITANIC

Music and Lyrics by
MAURY YESTON

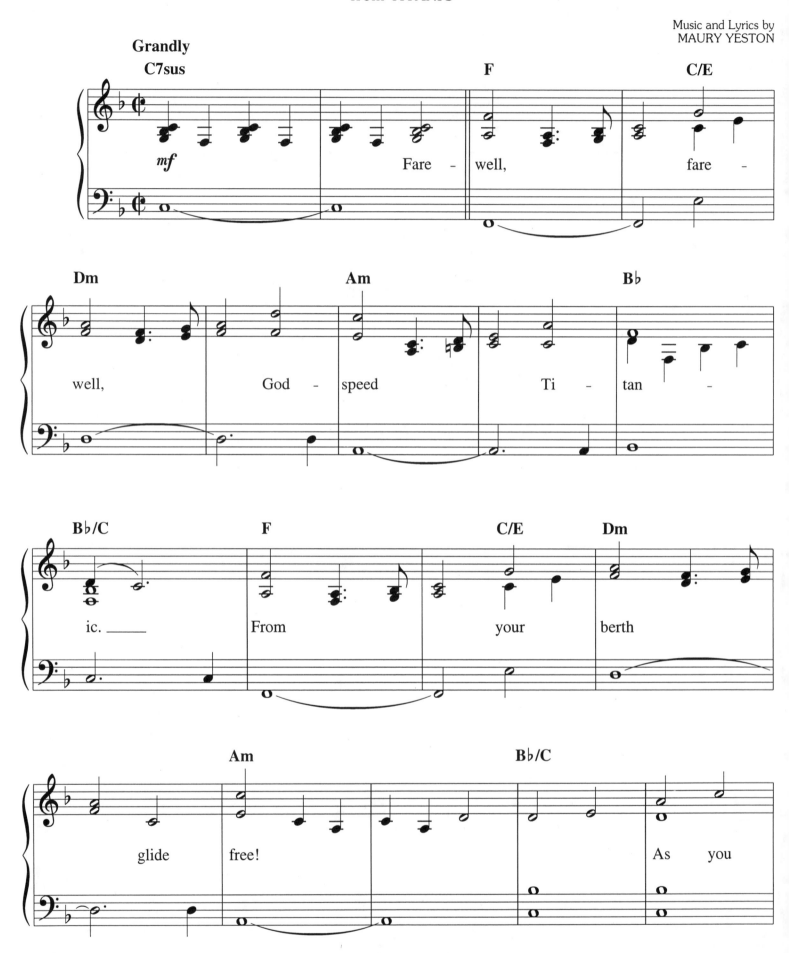

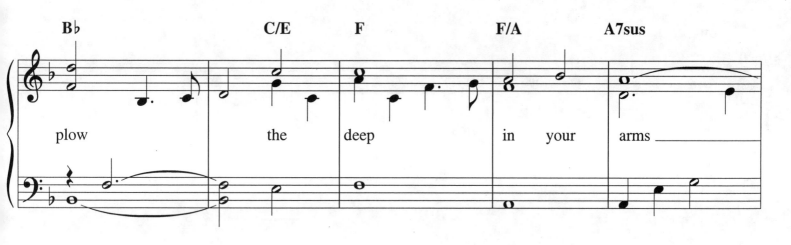

plow   the   deep   in   your   arms _____

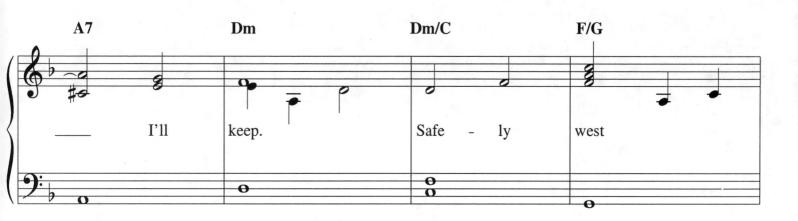

_____   I'll   keep.   Safe - ly   west

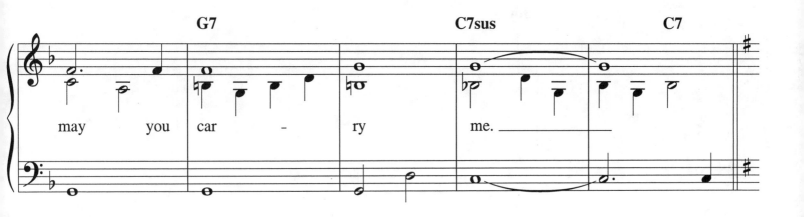

may   you   car   -   ry   me. _____

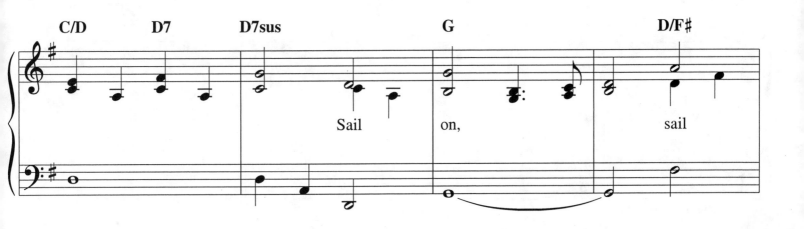

Sail   on,   sail

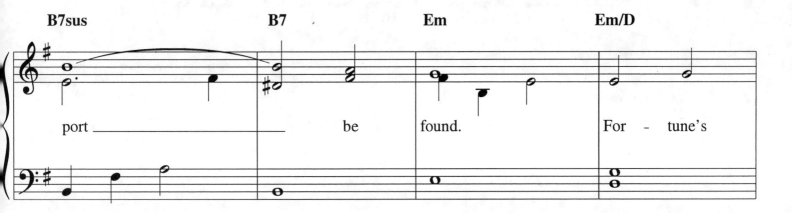

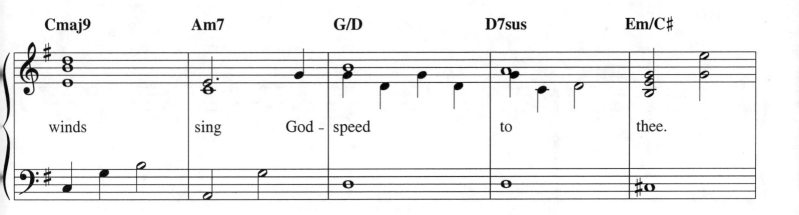

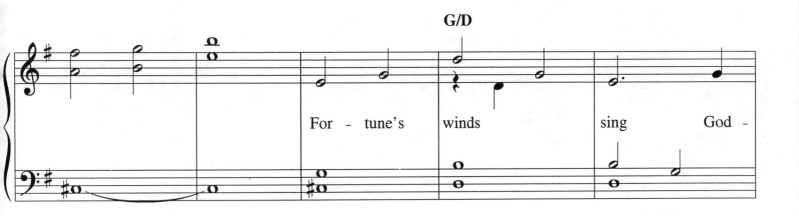

HELLO, YOUNG LOVERS
from THE KING AND I

Lyrics by OSCAR HAMMERSTEIN II
Music by RICHARD RODGERS

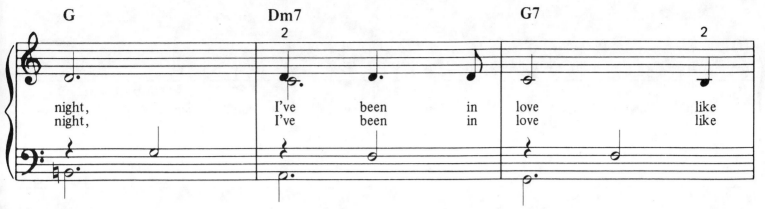

G   Dm7   G7

night,
night,   I've been in love   like
I've been in love   like

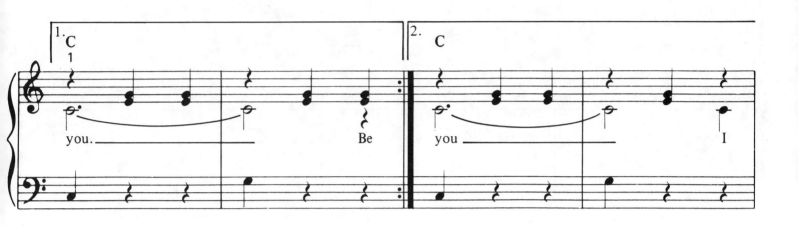

1. C   2. C

you. _____   Be   you _____   I

F   Gm7   F/A   Gm7

know how it   feels to have   wings on your   heels and to

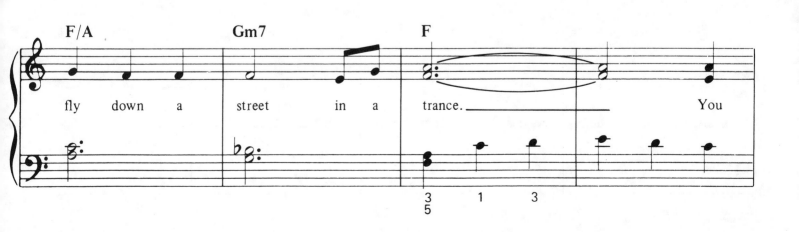

F/A   Gm7   F

fly down a   street in a   trance. _____   You

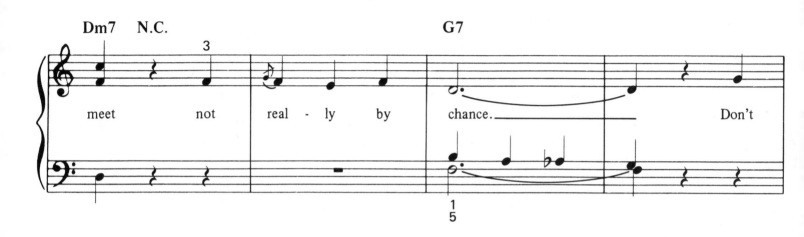

All of my mem - 'ries are hap - py to - night,

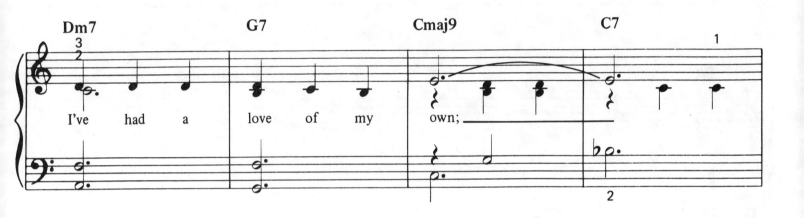

I've had a love of my own;

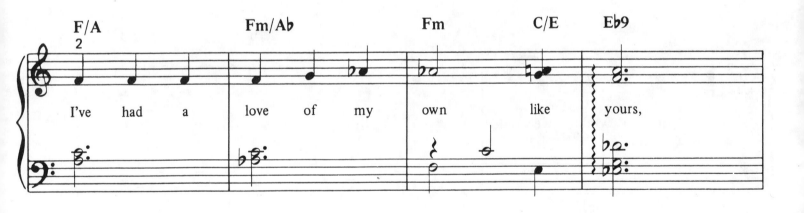

I've had a love of my own like yours,

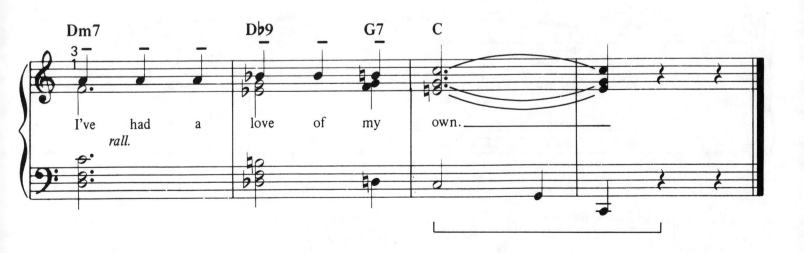

I've had a love of my own.

rall.

I WILL NEVER LEAVE YOU

from SIDE SHOW

Words by BILL RUSSELL
Music by HENRY KRIEGER

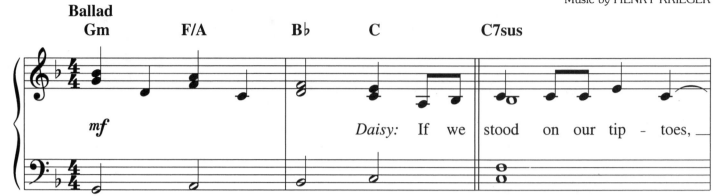

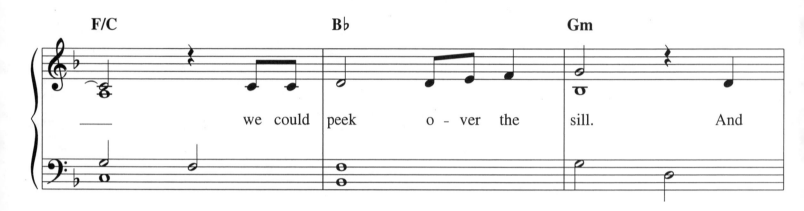

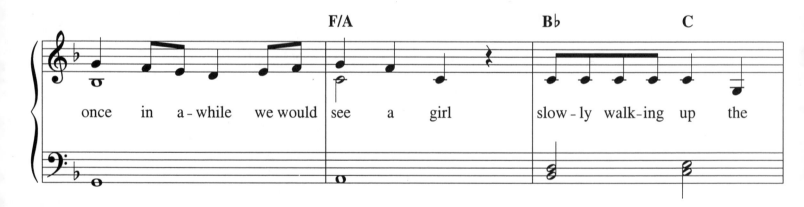

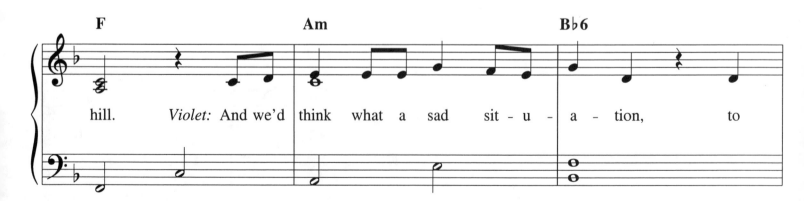

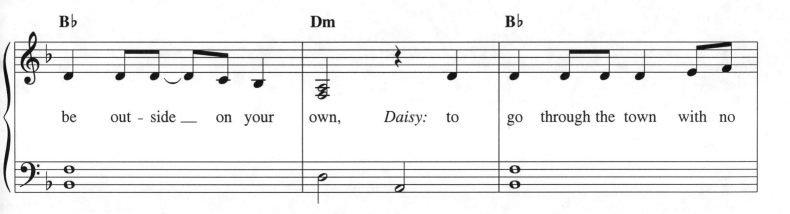

be out - side __ on your own, *Daisy:* to go through the town with no

play – mate, *Violet:* to go through life all a - lone. *Both:* I will nev - er

leave you. I will nev - er go a - way. __

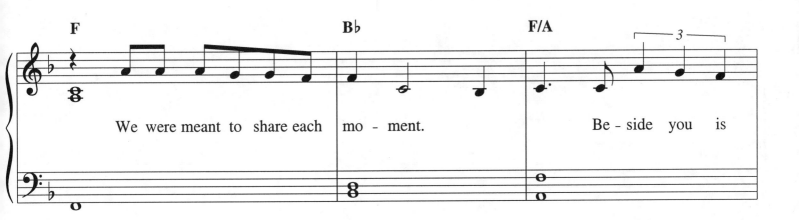

We were meant to share each mo - ment. Be - side you is

Gm

where I will stay.

A **Dm**

Ev - er - more and

Dm/C

al - ways,

G7sus

we'll be one tho' we're two.

G7

Gm **F/A**

For I will

B♭ **C** **F**

nev - er leave you.

C7sus

Daisy: When the day is filled with

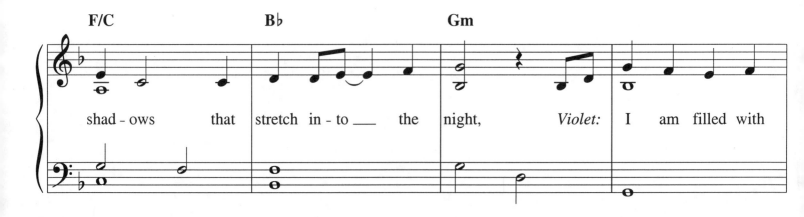

F/C

shad - ows that

B♭

stretch in - to ___ the night,

Gm

Violet: I am filled with

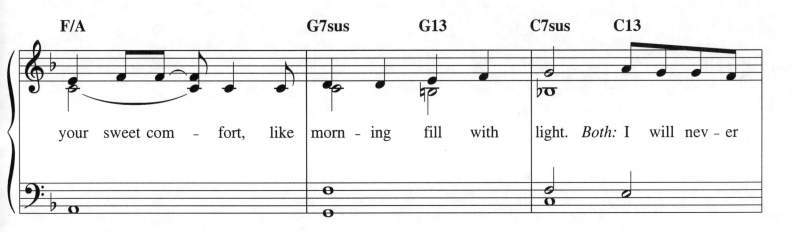

your sweet com - fort, like morn - ing fill with light. *Both:* I will nev - er

leave you, I will nev - er go a - way. __

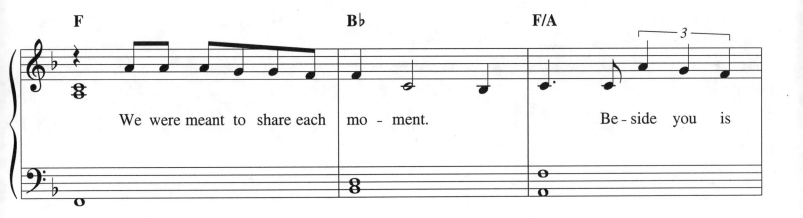

We were meant to share each mo - ment. Be - side you is

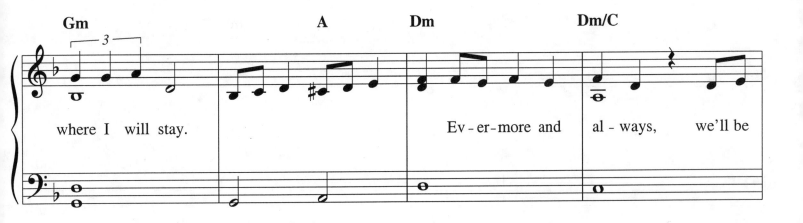

where I will stay. Ev - er-more and al - ways, we'll be

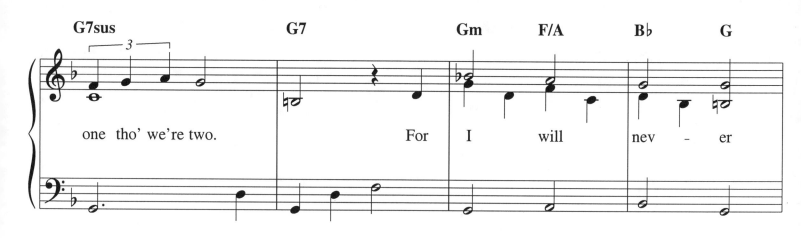

one tho' we're two. For I will nev – er

leave you. *Daisy:* I will nev – er leave you.

Both: I will nev – er go a – way. __ We were meant to share each

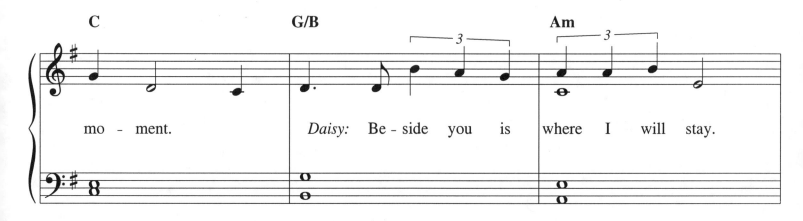

mo – ment. *Daisy:* Be – side you is where I will stay.

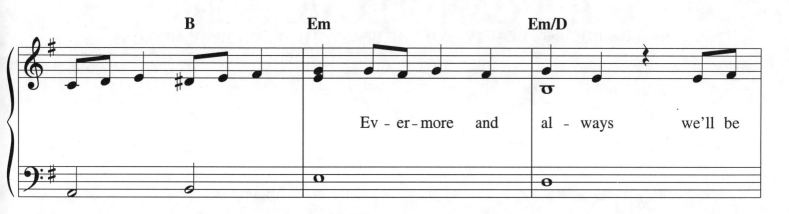

Ev - er - more and al - ways we'll be

one tho' we're two. For I will

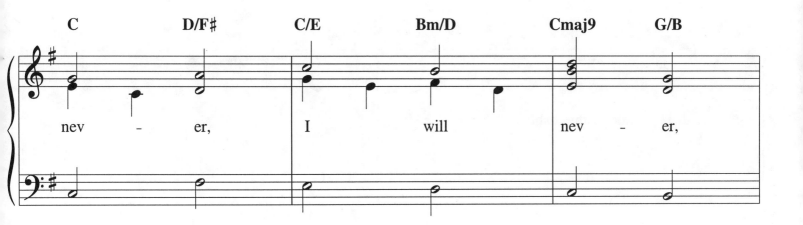

nev - er, I will nev - er,

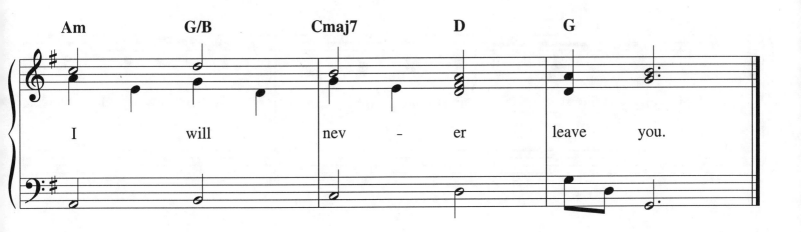

I will nev - er leave you.

IF I CAN'T LOVE HER
from Walt Disney's BEAUTY AND THE BEAST: THE BROADWAY MUSICAL

Music by ALAN MENKEN
Lyrics by TIM RICE

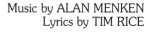

Beast: And in my twist-ed face ___

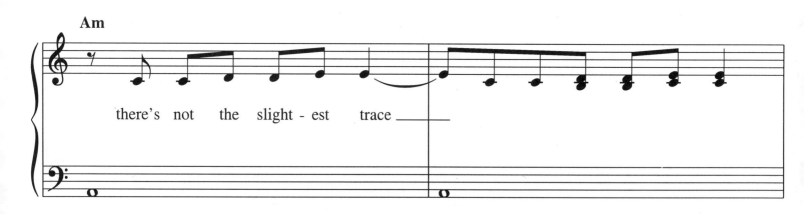

there's not the slight-est trace ___

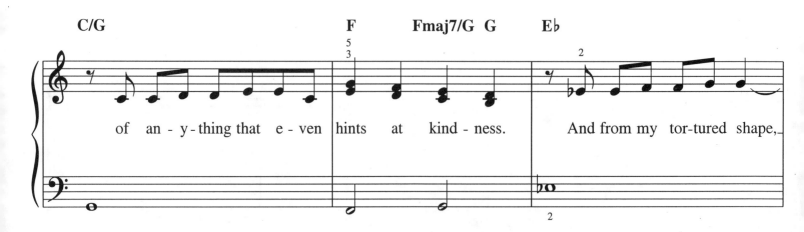

of an-y-thing that e-ven hints at kind-ness. And from my tor-tured shape,

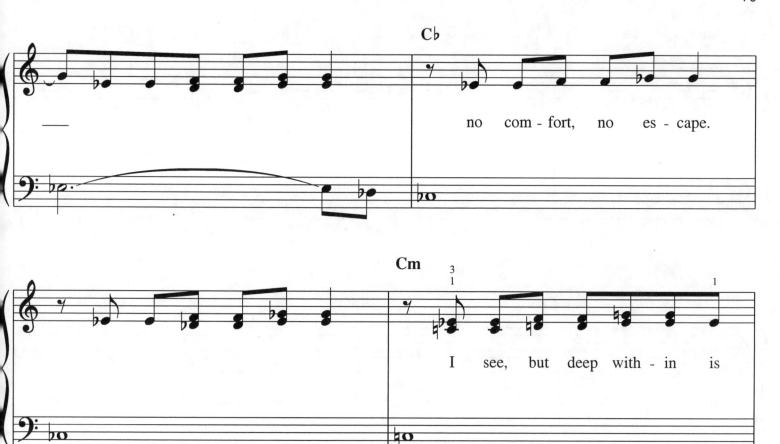

Cb

no com - fort, no es - cape.

Cm

I see, but deep with - in is

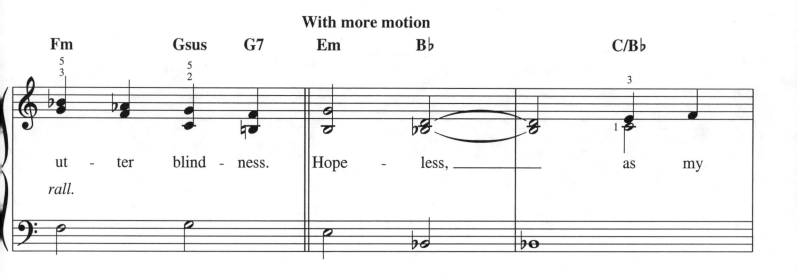

With more motion

Fm   Gsus   G7   Em   Bb   C/Bb

ut - ter   blind - ness.   Hope - less, _____   as my

rall.

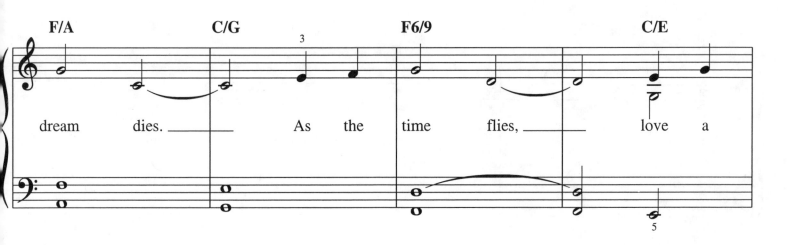

F/A   C/G   F6/9   C/E

dream   dies. _____   As the   time   flies, _____   love   a

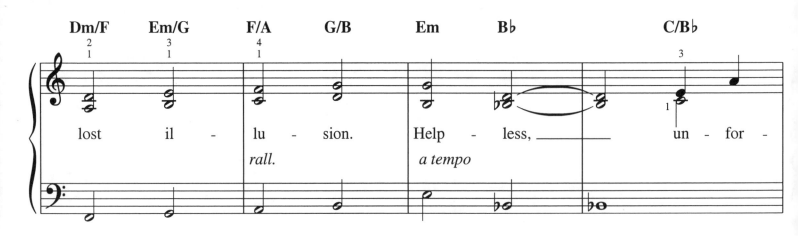

lost il - lu - sion. Help - less, _____ un - for -

rall.   *a tempo*

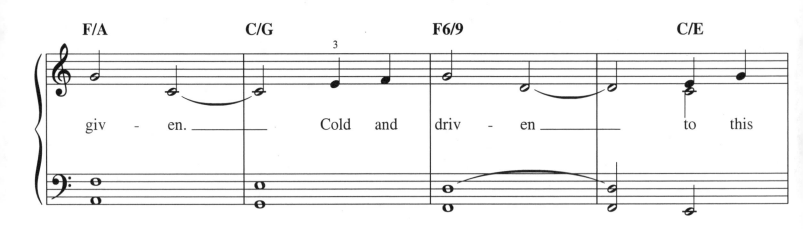

giv - en. _____ Cold and driv - en _____ to this

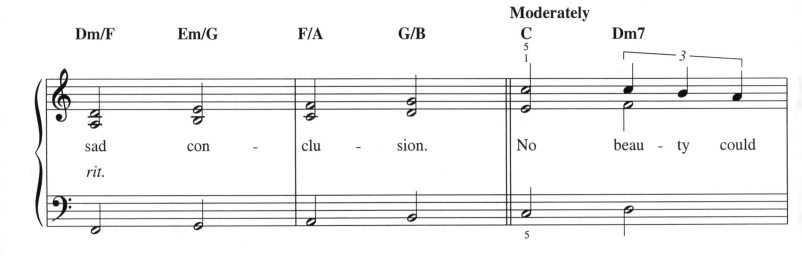

sad con - clu - sion. No beau - ty could

rit.

Moderately

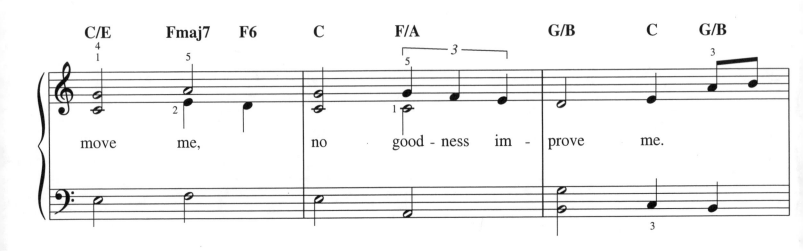

move me, no good - ness im - prove me.

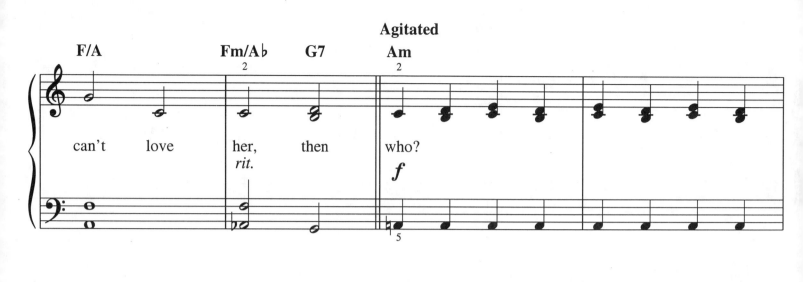

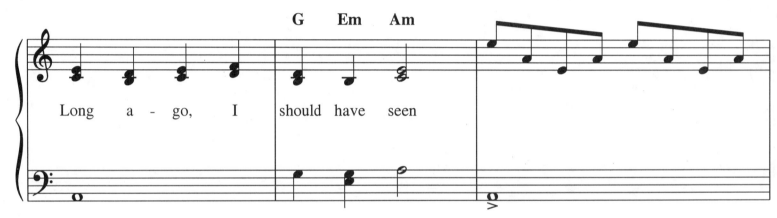

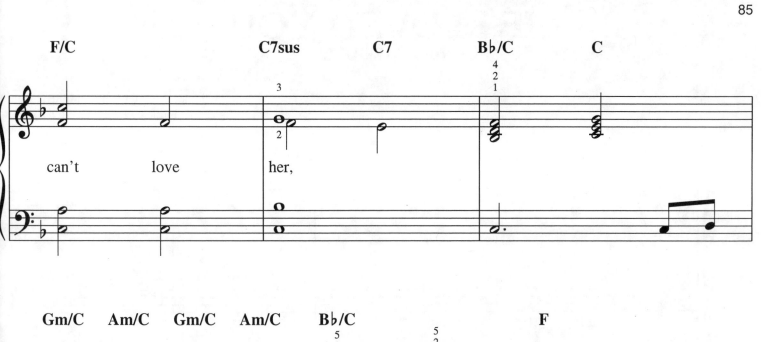

F/C   C7sus   C7   Bb/C   C

can't   love   her,

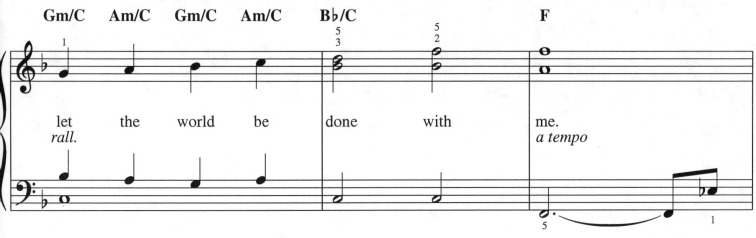

Gm/C   Am/C   Gm/C   Am/C   Bb/C   F

let   the   world   be   done   with   me.
rall.   *a tempo*

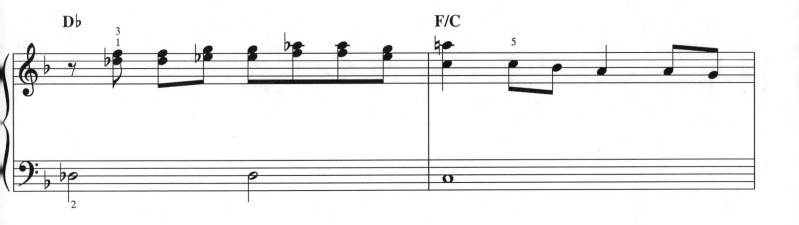

Db   F/C

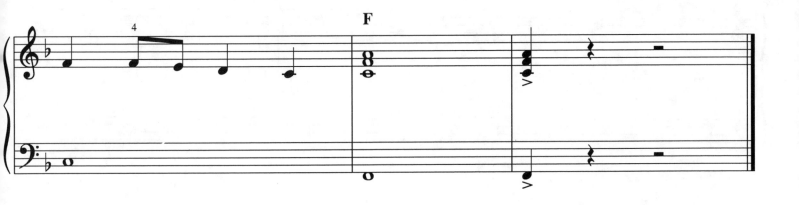

F

IF I LOVED YOU
from CAROUSEL

Lyrics by OSCAR HAMMERSTEIN II
Music by RICHARD RODGERS

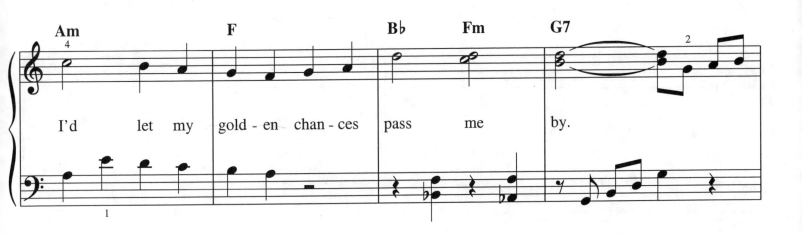

Soon you'd leave me. Off you would go in the

mist of day, nev - er, nev - er to know

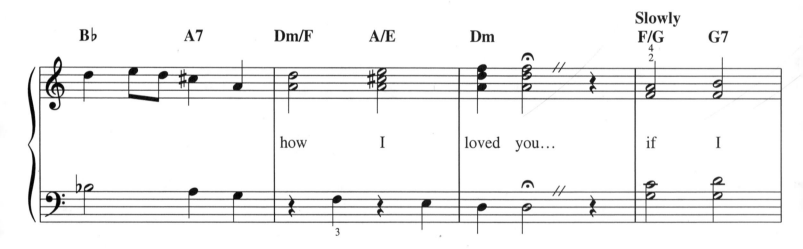

how I loved you... if I

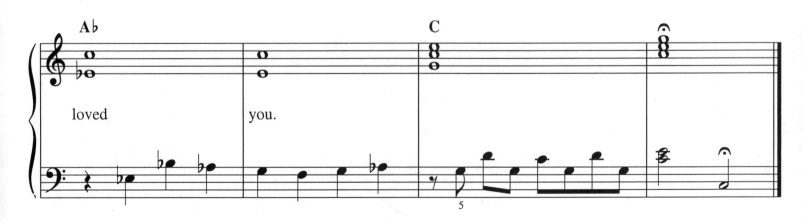

loved you.

THE LAST NIGHT OF THE WORLD

from MISS SAIGON

Music by CLAUDE-MICHEL SCHÖNBERG
Lyrics by RICHARD MALTBY Jr. and ALAIN BOUBLIL
Adapted from original French Lyrics by ALAIN BOUBLIL

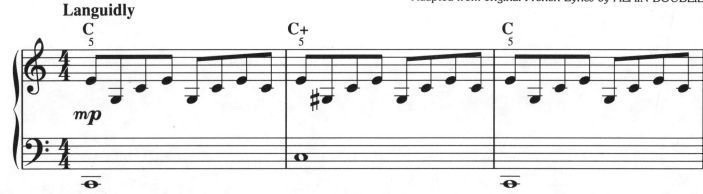

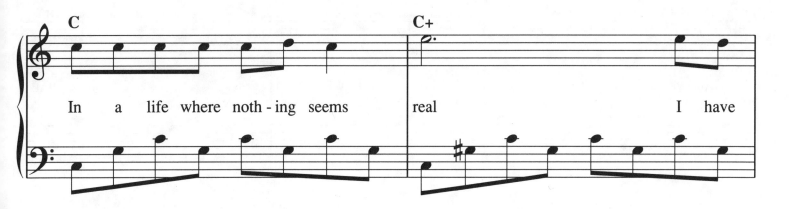

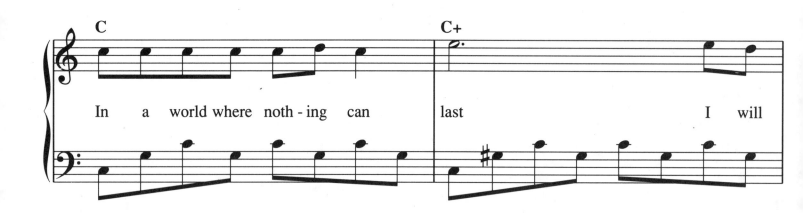

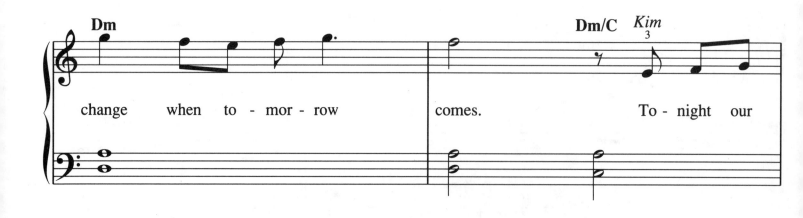

91

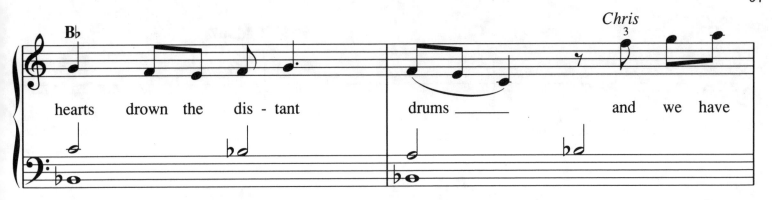

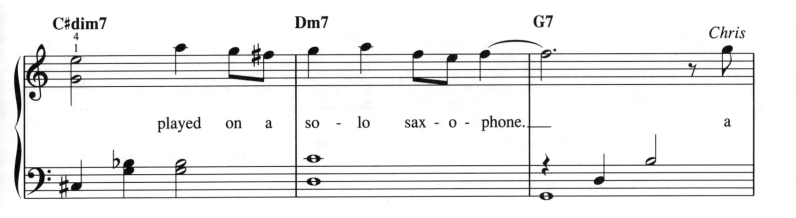

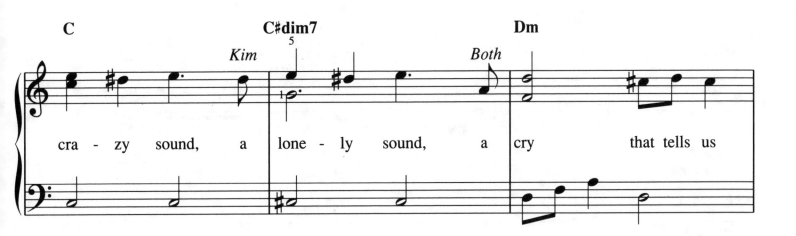

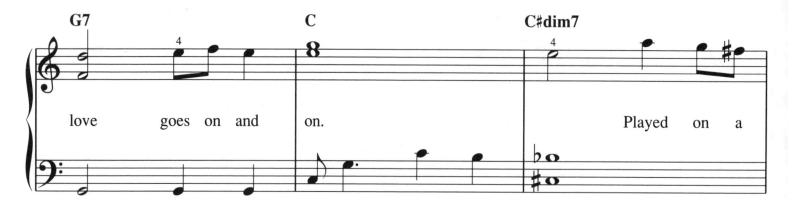

G7 **C** **C#dim7**

love   goes on and   on.   Played   on   a

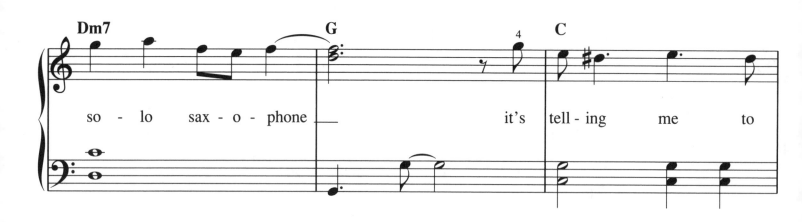

Dm7 **G** **C**

so - lo sax - o - phone ___   it's tell - ing   me   to

C#dim7 **Dm7** **G7**

hold   you tight   and   dance   like it's the   last ___   night   of the

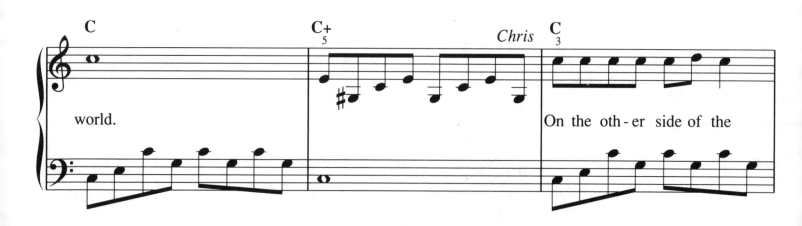

C **C+** *Chris* **C**

world.   On the oth - er side of the

C+ earth   **C** there's a place where life still has   **C+** worth. I will

Fmaj7 take you._____   **F/G** *Kim* I'll go with   **C** *Chris* you.____ You won't be -

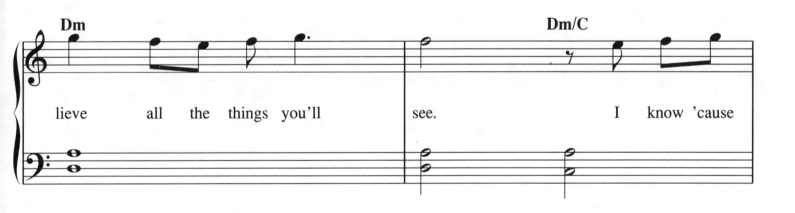

Dm lieve all the things you'll   see.   **Dm/C** I know 'cause

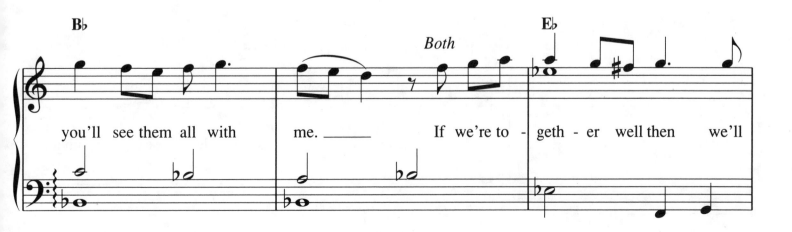

B♭ you'll see them all with   me._____ *Both* If we're to - geth - er well then   **E♭** we'll

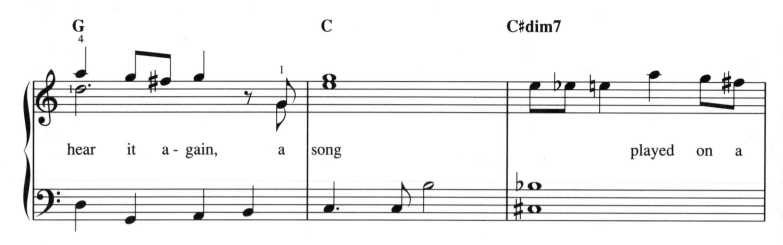

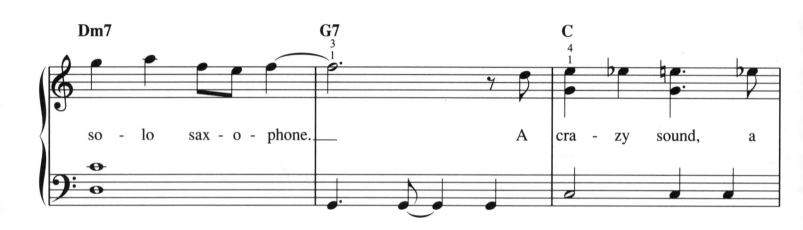

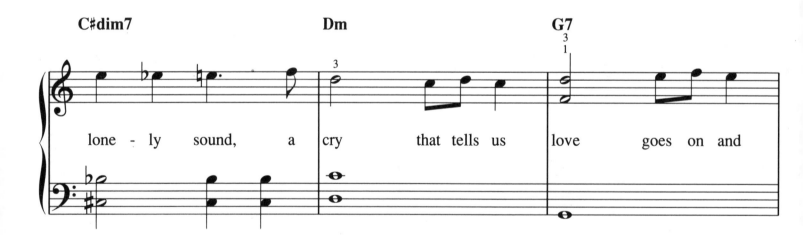

It's tell-ing me to hold you tight and

dance like it's the last night of the world.

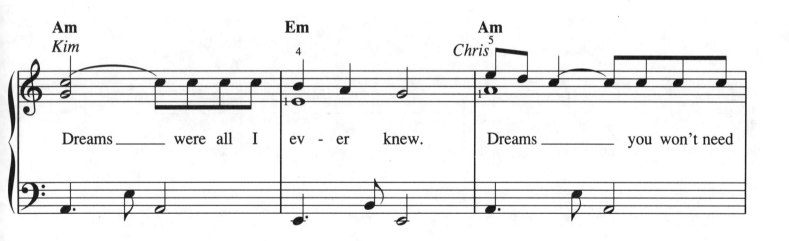

Kim Dreams ___ were all I ev-er knew. *Chris* Dreams ___ you won't need

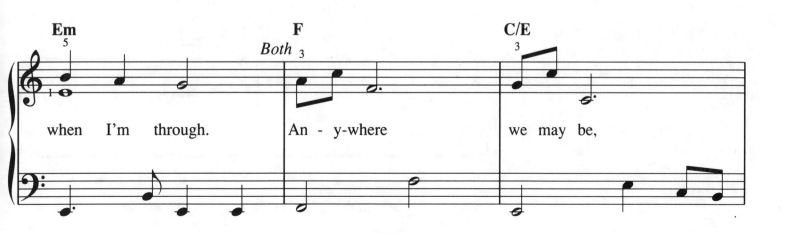

when I'm through. *Both* An-y-where we may be,

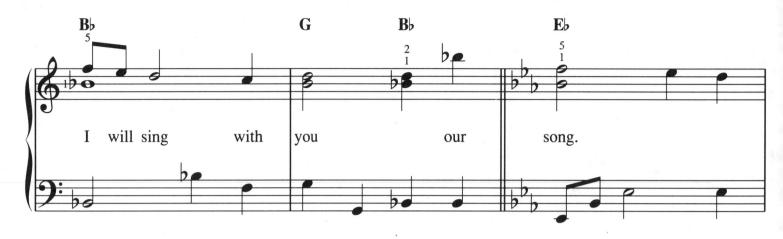

I will sing with you our song.

So

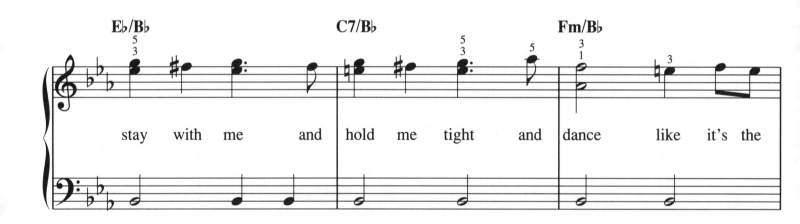

stay with me and hold me tight and dance like it's the

last night of the world. _____

KANSAS CITY
from SMOKEY JOE'S CAFE

Words and Music by JERRY LEIBER
and MIKE STOLLER

come. They got a cra-zy way of lov-in' there and

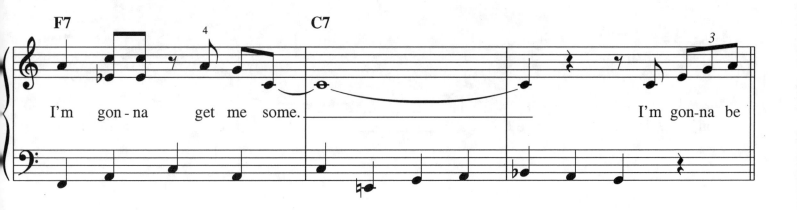

I'm gon-na get me some. I'm gon-na be

stand-in' on the cor-ner Twelfth Street and Vine.
Pack my clothes, _ leave at the crack of dawn.

I'm gon-na be stand-in' on the cor-ner Twelfth Street and Vine, _
I'm go-ing to pack my clothes, _ leave at the crack of dawn.

with my Kan-sas Cit-y ba-by and a
My old la-dy will be sleep-in' an' she

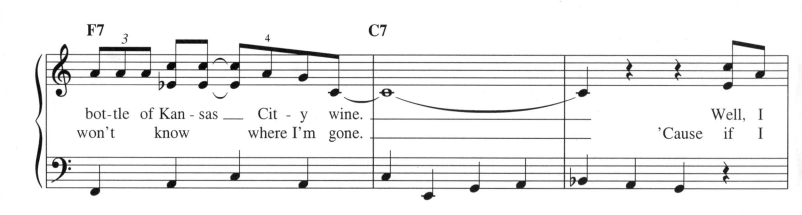

bot-tle of Kan-sas __ Cit-y wine. __ Well, I
won't know where I'm gone. __ 'Cause if I

might take a train, __ I might take a plane, __ but if I have to walk I'm
stay with that wom - an I know I'm gon-na die, got-ta find a brand new ba-by and

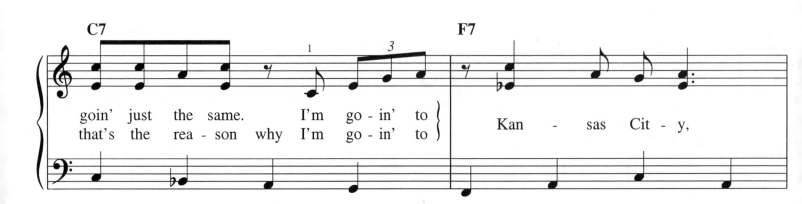

goin' just the same. I'm go-in' to
that's the rea-son why I'm go-in' to Kan - sas Cit-y,

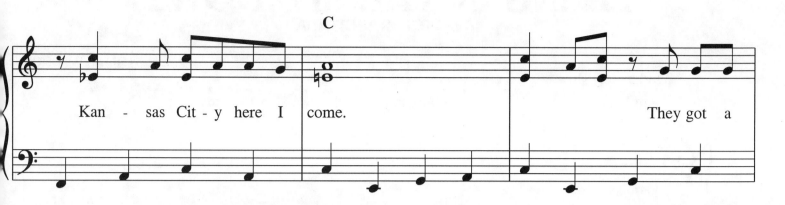

Kan - sas Cit - y here I come. They got a

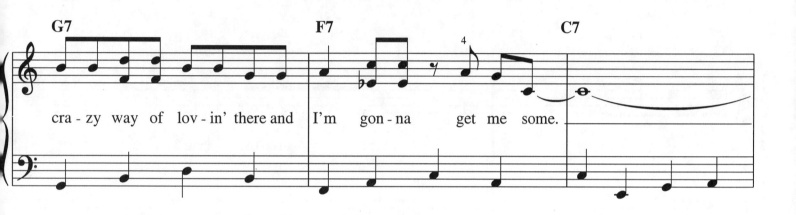

cra - zy way of lov - in' there and I'm gon - na get me some.

1. I'm go-in' to 2. They got a cra - zy way of lov - in' there and

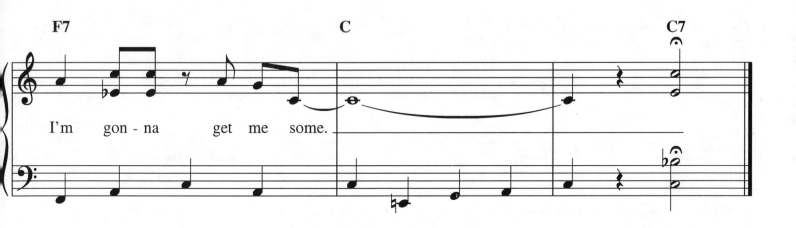

I'm gon - na get me some.

LIVING IN THE SHADOWS

from VICTOR/VICTORIA

Words by LESLIE BRICUSSE
Music by FRANK WILDHORN

Moderately slow

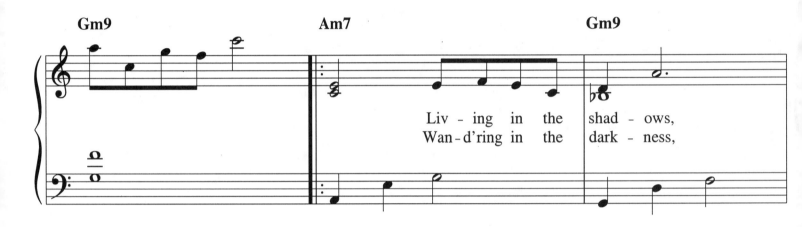

Liv – ing in the shad – ows,
Wan – d'ring in the dark – ness,

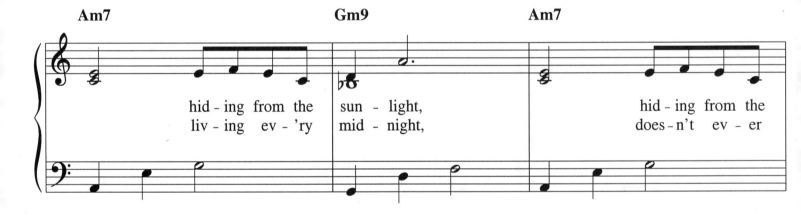

hid – ing from the sun – light,
liv – ing ev – 'ry mid – night,

hid – ing from the
does – n't ev – er

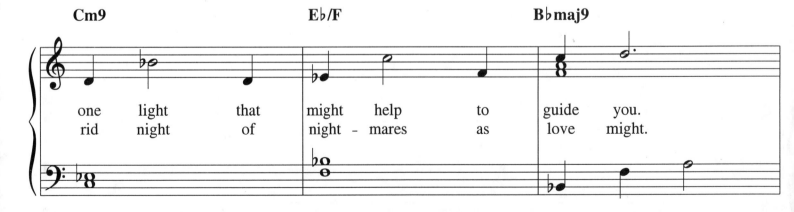

one light that might help to guide you.
rid night of night – mares as love might.

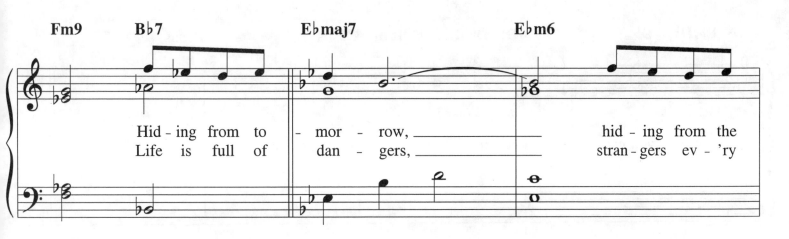

Hid - ing from to - mor - row, _____ hid - ing from the
Life is full of dan - gers, _____ stran - gers ev - 'ry

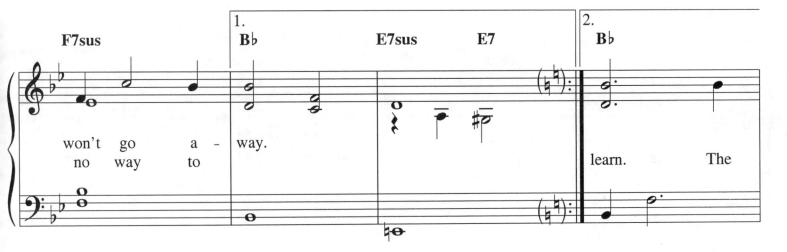

day, _____ on - ly brings a sor - row that
turn. _____ Liv - ing in the shad - ows, there's

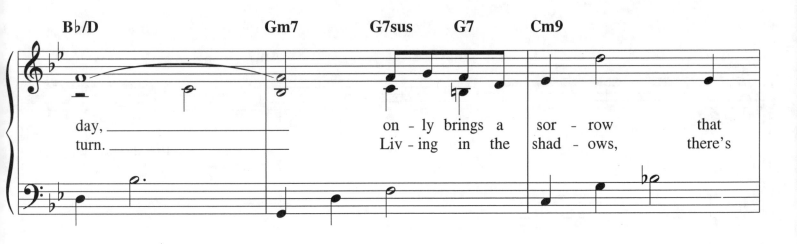

won't go a - way.
no way to

learn. The

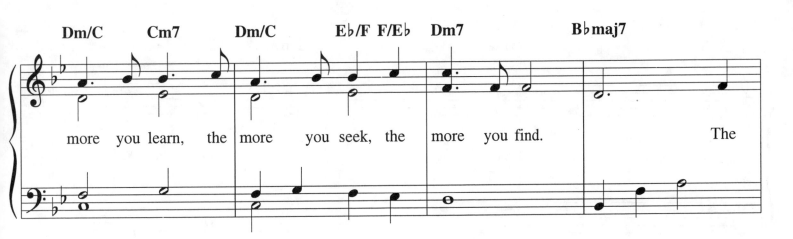

more you learn, the more you seek, the more you find.

The

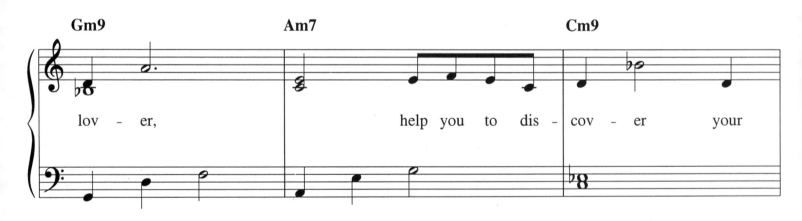

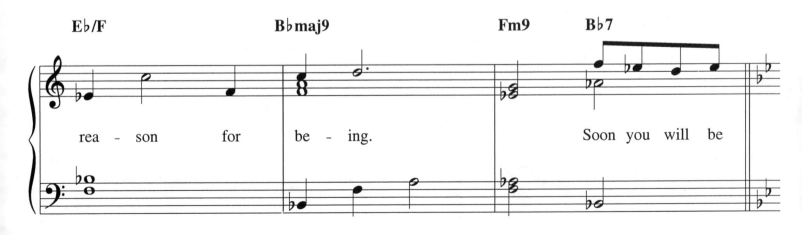

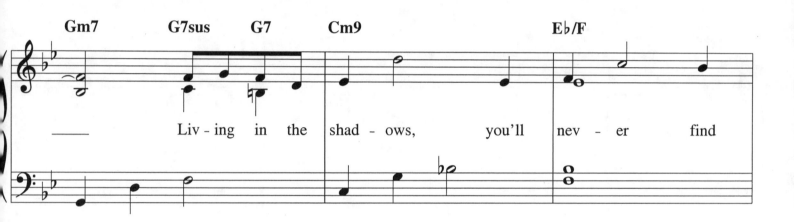

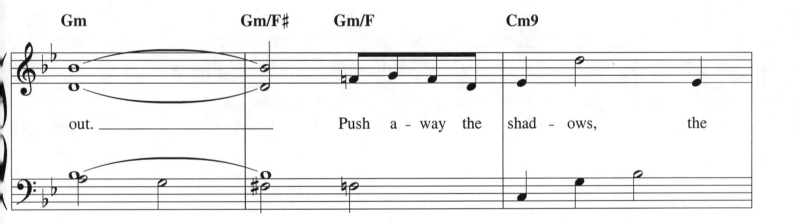

LOVE POTION NUMBER 9
from SMOKEY JOE'S CAFE

Words and Music by JERRY LEIBER
and MIKE STOLLER

Moderately bright

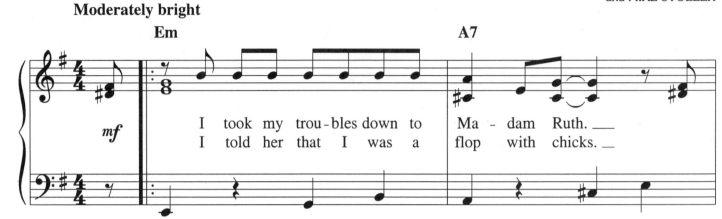

I took my trou-bles down to a Ma-dam Ruth. ___
I told her that I was a flop with chicks. ___

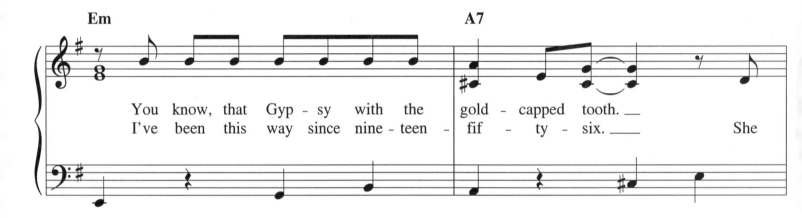

You know, that Gyp-sy with the gold-capped tooth. ___
I've been this way since nine-teen - fif - ty - six. ___ She

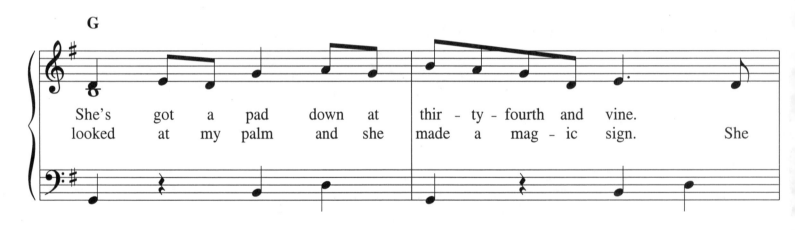

She's got a pad down at thir-ty-fourth and vine.
looked at my palm and she made a mag-ic sign. She

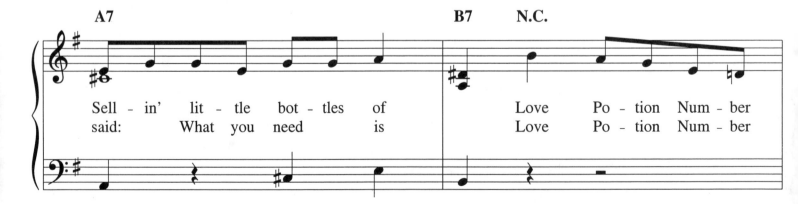

Sell-in' lit-tle bot-tles of Love Po-tion Num-ber
said: What you need is Love Po-tion Num-ber

A7

smelled like tur – pen – tine and looked like In – di – a ink. ___ I

B **N.C.**

held my nose; I closed my eyes; I took a drink.

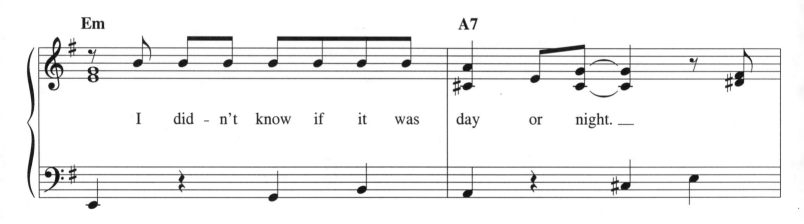

Em **A7**

I did – n't know if it was day or night. __

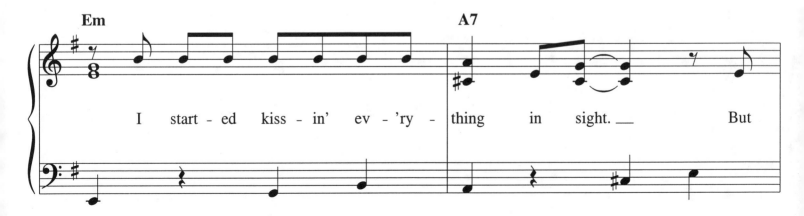

Em **A7**

I start – ed kiss – in' ev – 'ry – thing in sight. __ But

when I kissed the cop down at Thir - ty - fourth and Vine, he

broke my lit – tle bot – tle of Love Po – tion Num – ber

1.

Nine.

2.

Nine.

MAKE BELIEVE
from SHOW BOAT

Lyrics by OSCAR HAMMERSTEIN II
Music by JEROME KERN

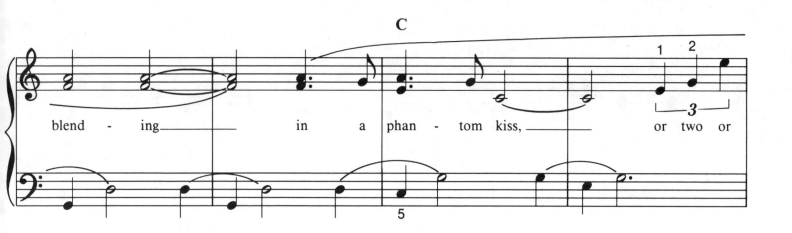

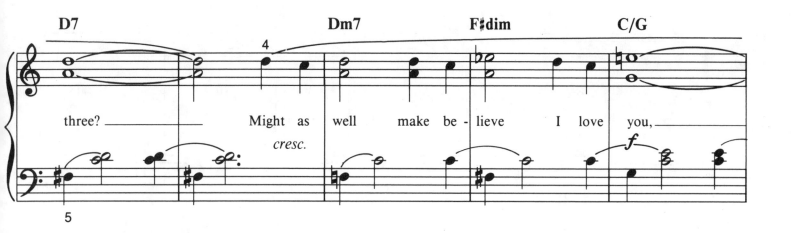

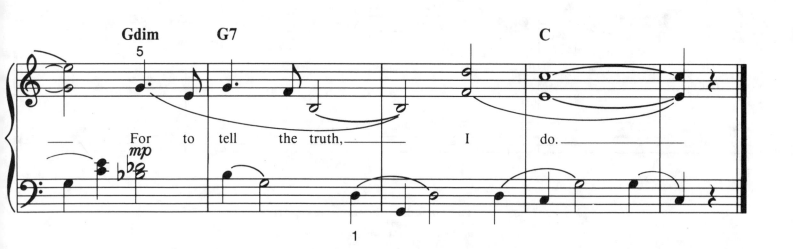

MY OWN BEST FRIEND
from CHICAGO

Words by FRED EBB
Music by JOHN KANDER

Slow and proud

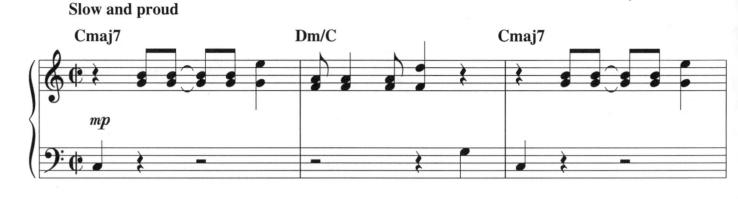

One thing I know,
Ba - by's a - live,

and
but

I've al-ways known,
ba-by's a - lone,

and

I am my own ___
and ba-by's { her / his } own ___

best
best

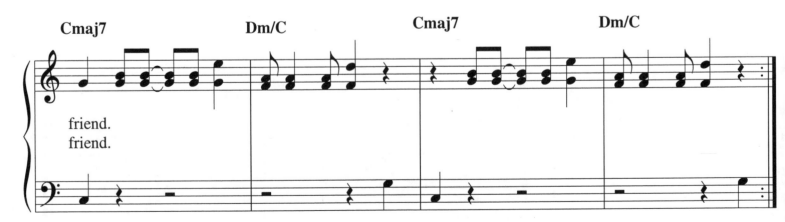

friend.
friend.

Man - y's the {guy / girl} who told me {he / she} cares,

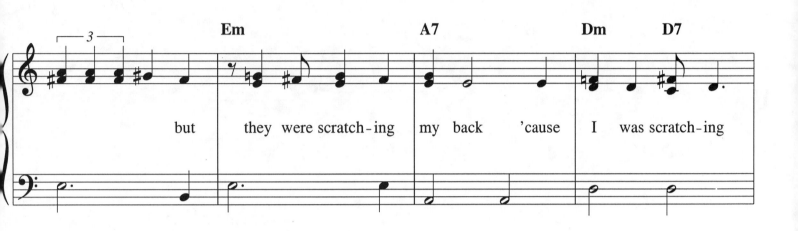

but they were scratch-ing my back 'cause I was scratch-ing

theirs. And If

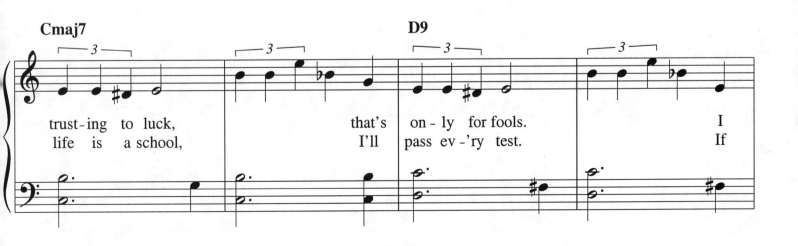

trust-ing to luck, that's on - ly for fools. I
life is a school, I'll pass ev-'ry test. If

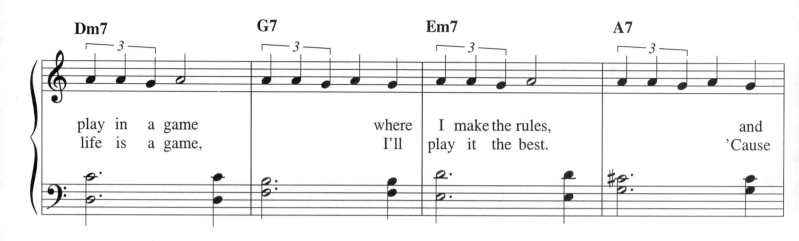

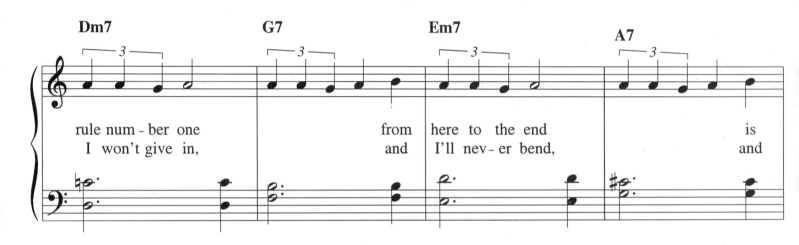

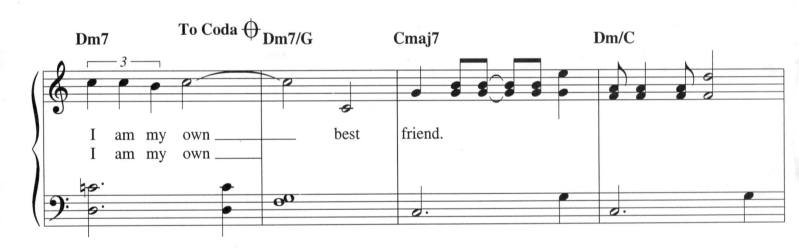

A NEW LIFE
from JEKYLL & HYDE

Words by LESLIE BRICUSSE
Music by FRANK WILDHORN

Moderately slow, freely

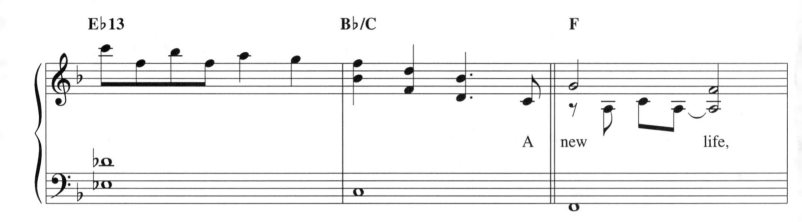

A new life,

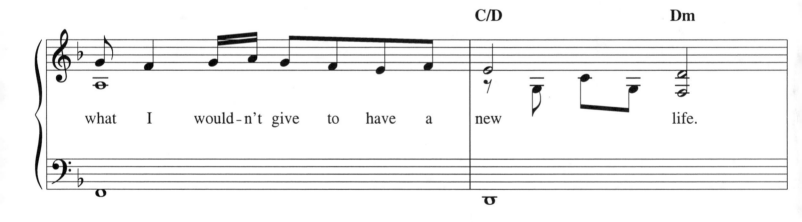

what I would-n't give to have a new life.

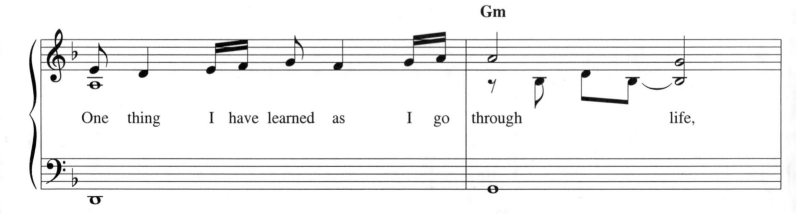

One thing I have learned as I go through life,

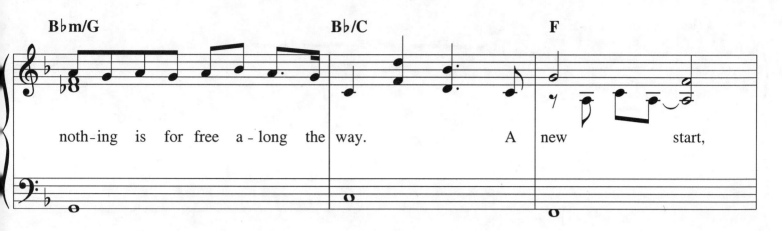

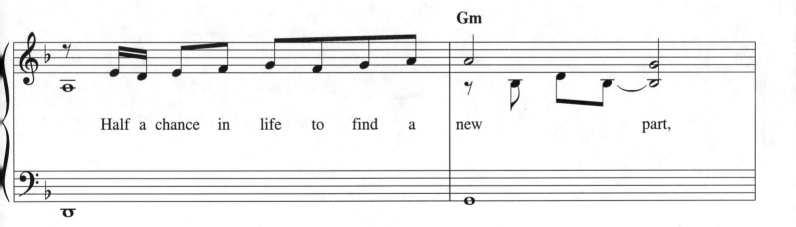

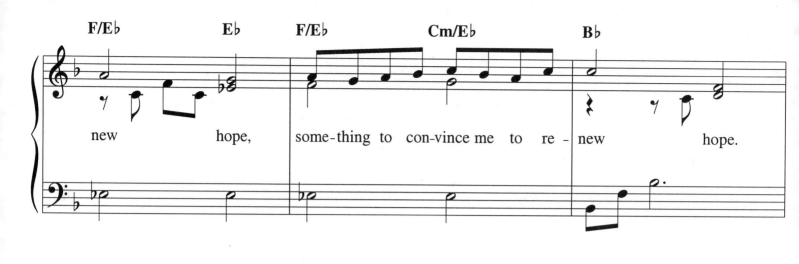

new hope, some-thing to con-vince me to re - new hope.

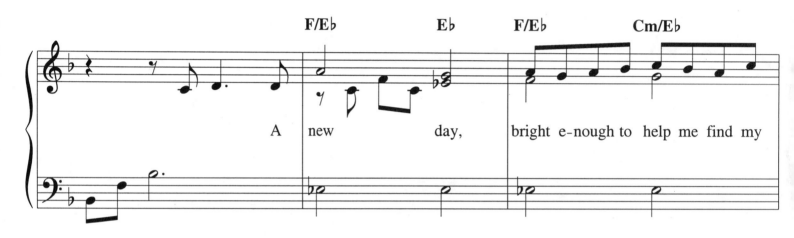

A new day, bright e-nough to help me find my

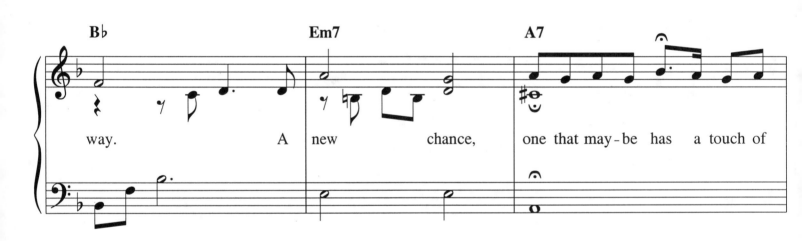

way. A new chance, one that may-be has a touch of

ro - mance. Where can it be, _____ the chance for

me? A new dream, I have one I know that ver - y

few dream. I would like to see that o - ver - due dream,

e - ven though it nev - er may come true. A new love,

though I know there's no such thing as true love. E - ven so, al - though I nev - er

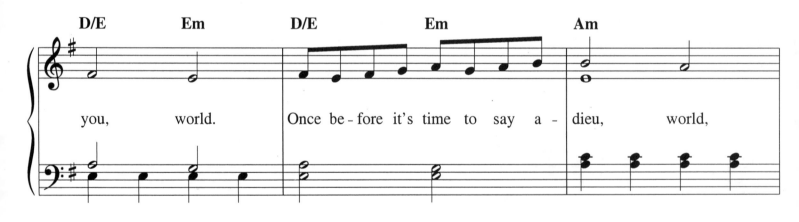

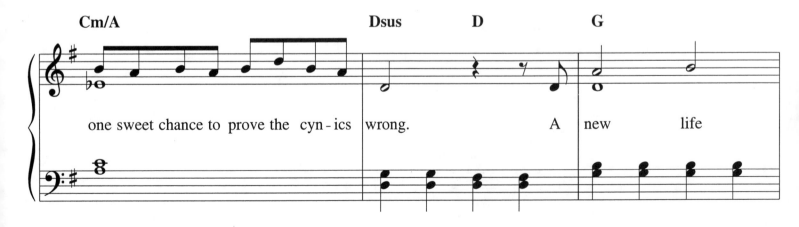

OL' MAN RIVER
from SHOW BOAT

Lyrics by OSCAR HAMMERSTEIN II
Music by JEROME KERN

Slowly (𝅗𝅥 = 1 count)

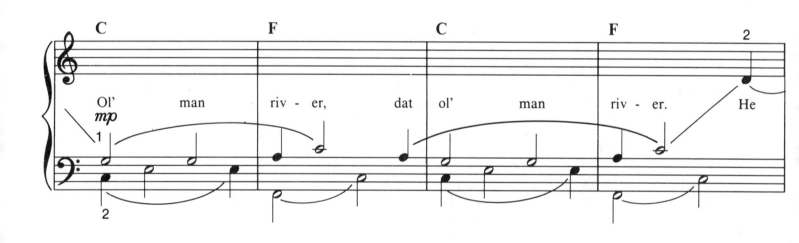

Ol' man riv-er, dat ol' man riv-er. He

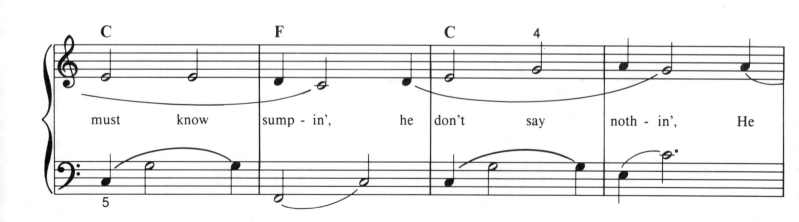

must know sump-in', he don't say noth-in', He

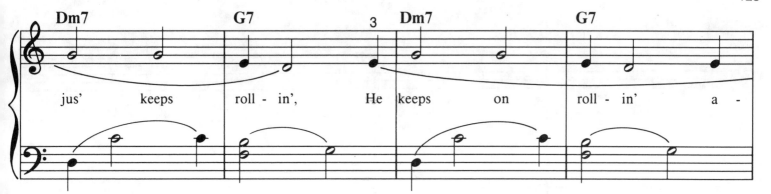

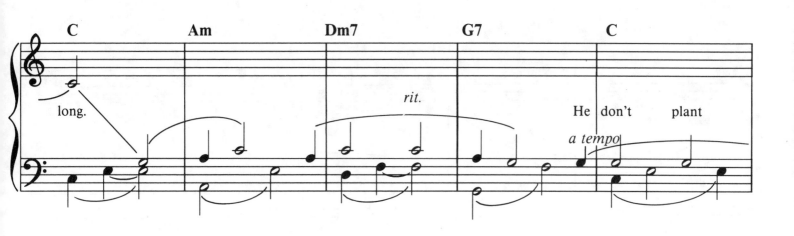

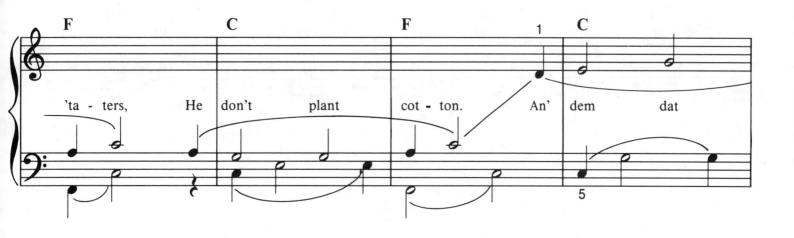

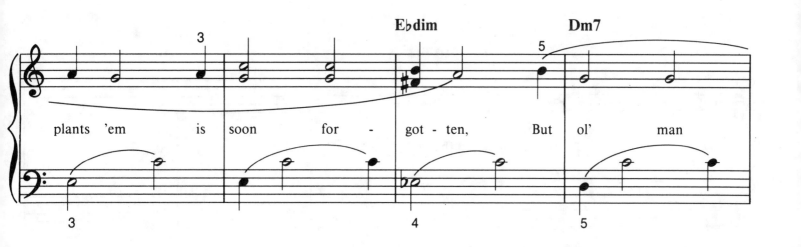

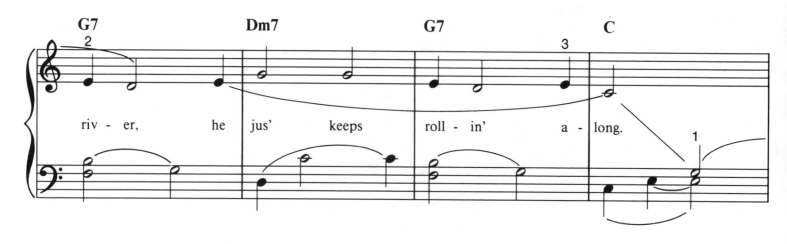

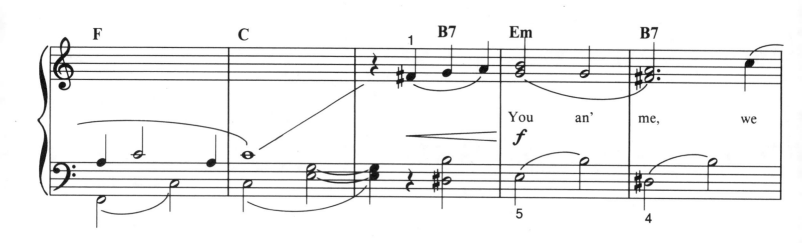

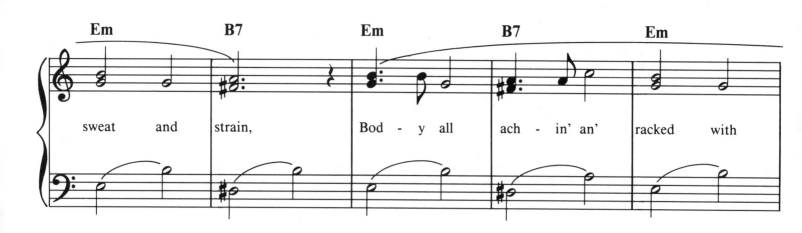

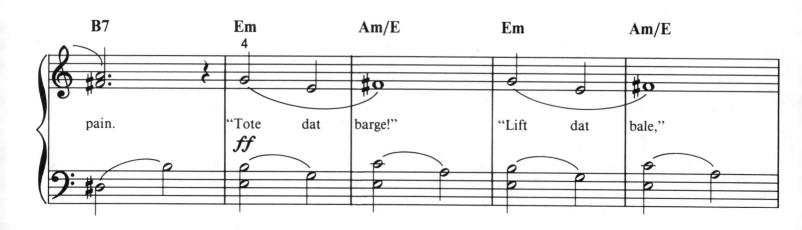

Git a lit - tle drunk an' you land in jail.

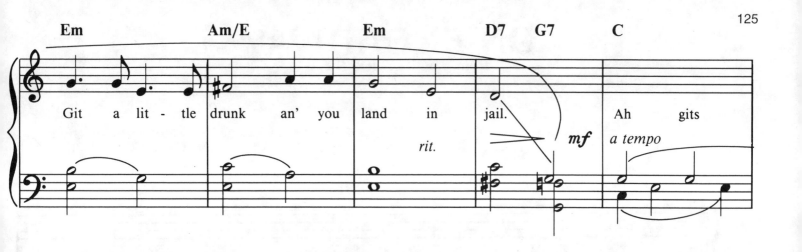

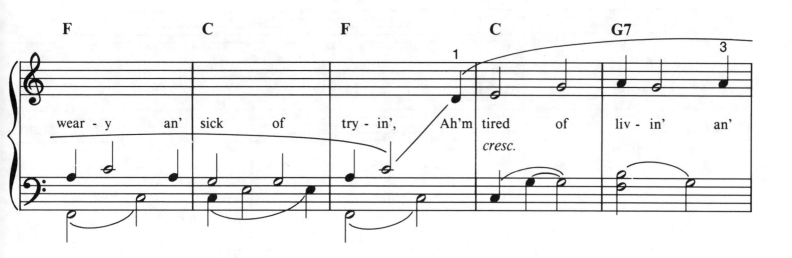

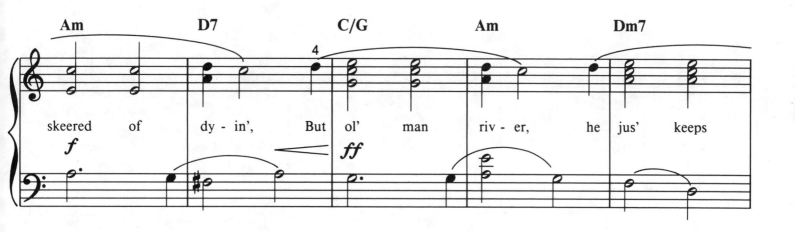

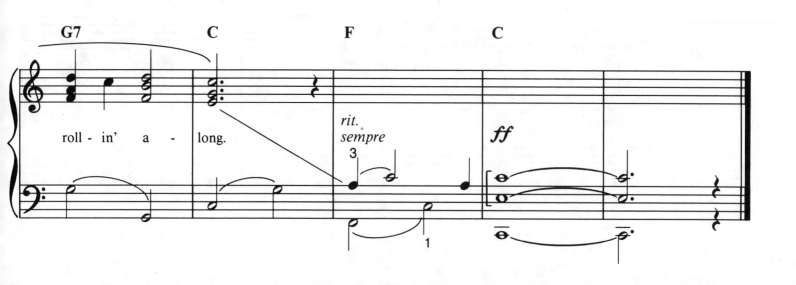

ON BROADWAY
from SMOKEY JOE'S CAFE

Words and Music by BARRY MANN, CYNTHIA WEIL,
MIKE STOLLER and JERRY LEIBER

SEASONS OF LOVE

from RENT

Words and Music by
JONATHAN LARSON

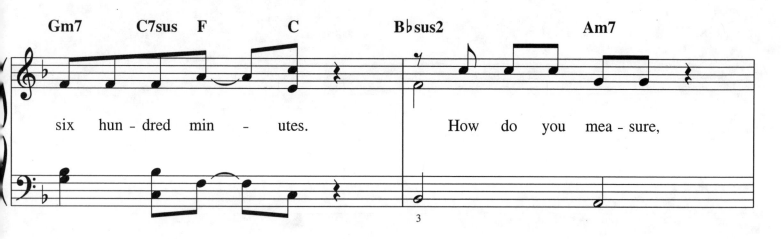

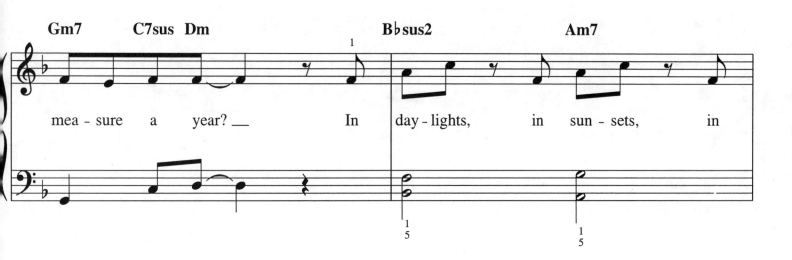

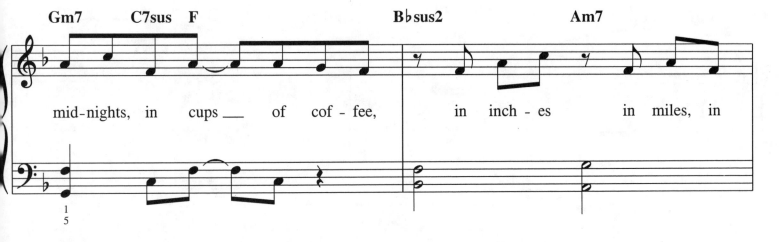

130

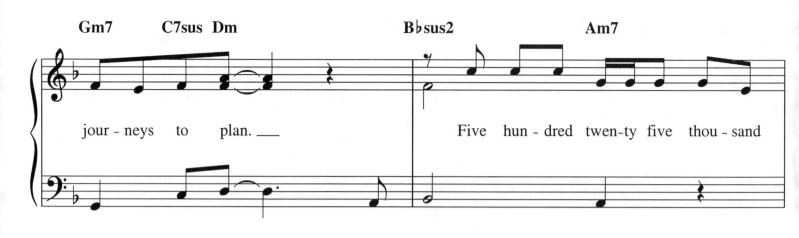

jour - neys   to   plan. ___   Five hun - dred twen-ty five thou - sand

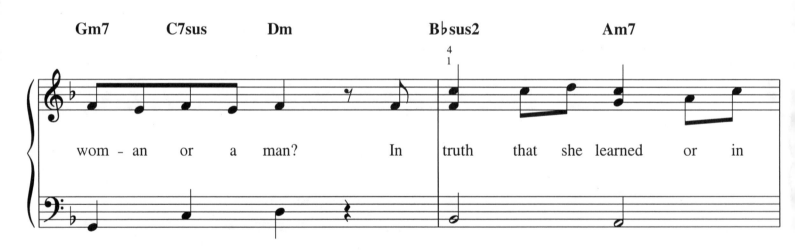

six hun - dred min - utes.   How   do   you mea - sure the life   of a

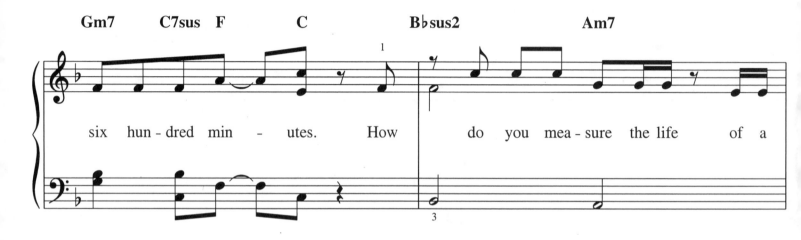

wom - an or a man?   In   truth   that   she learned   or   in

times   that   he cried, ___   in   bridg - es   he burned   or   the

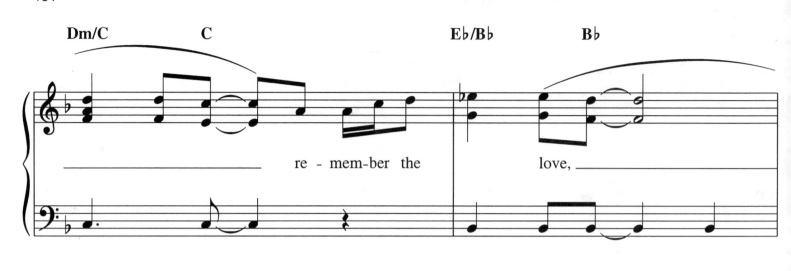

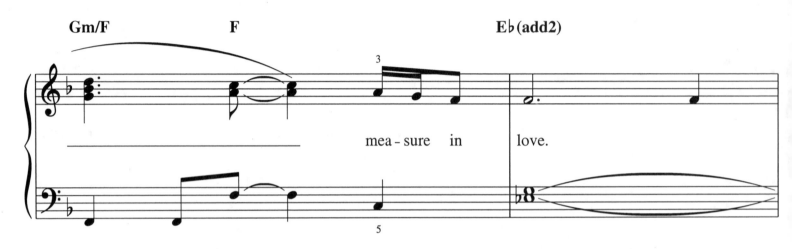

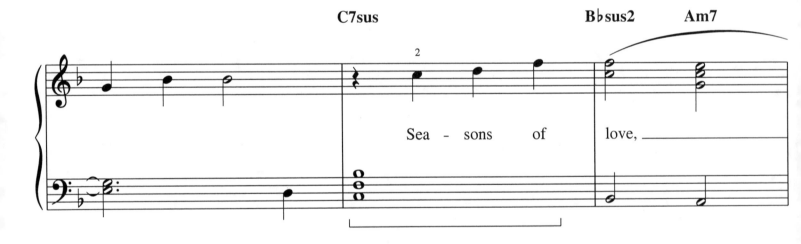

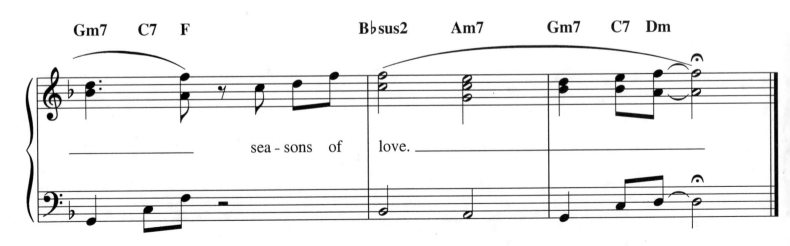

SOMETHING GOOD
from THE SOUND OF MUSIC

Lyrics and Music by
RICHARD RODGERS

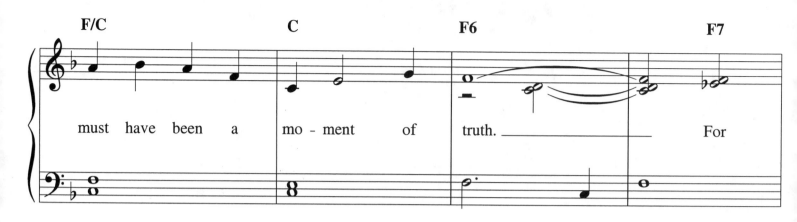

must have been a mo - ment of truth. _____ For

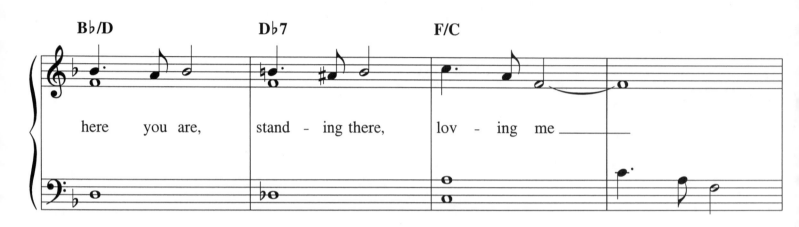

here you are, stand - ing there, lov - ing me _____

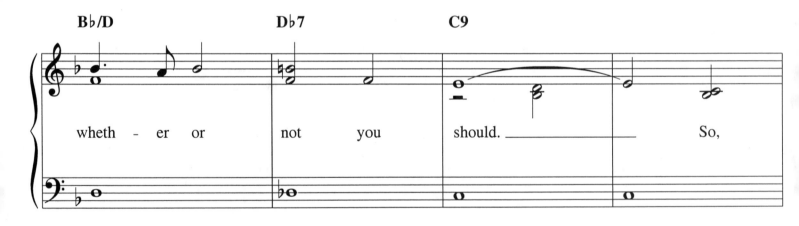

wheth - er or not you should. _____ So,

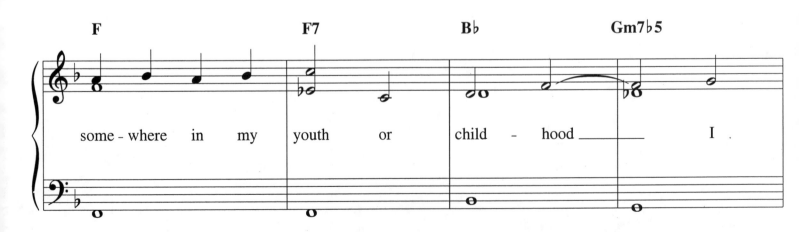

some - where in my youth or child - hood _____ I

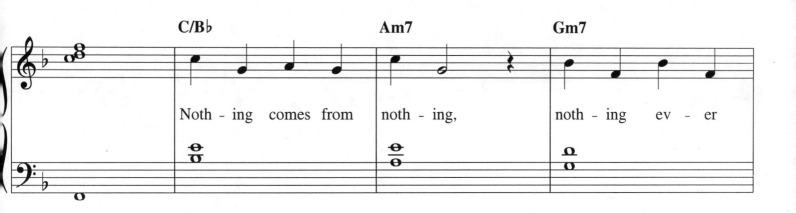

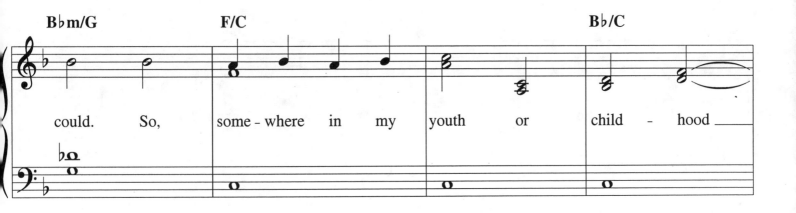

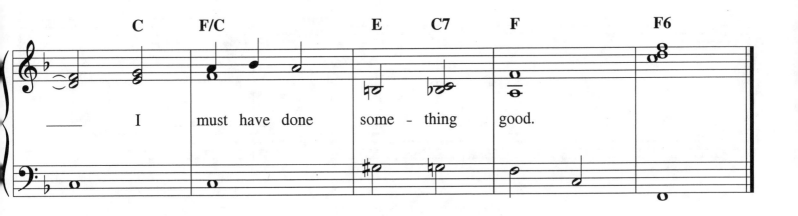

SHALL WE DANCE?
from THE KING AND I

Lyrics by OSCAR HAMMERSTEIN II
Music by RICHARD RODGERS

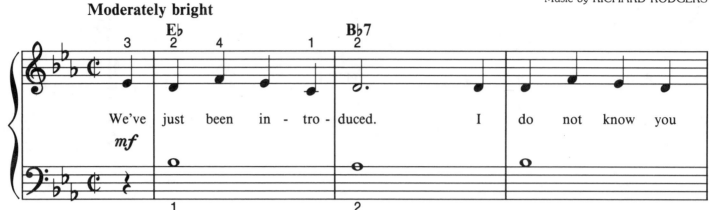

We've just been in - tro - duced. I do not know you

well. But when the mu - sic start - ed, some - thing

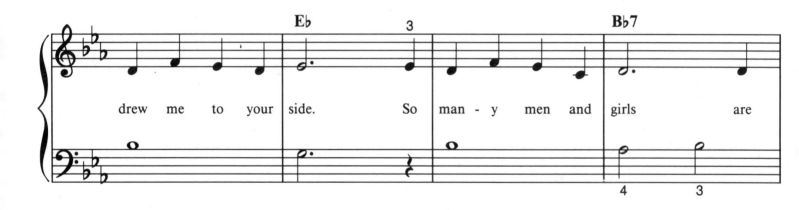

drew me to your side. So man - y men and girls are

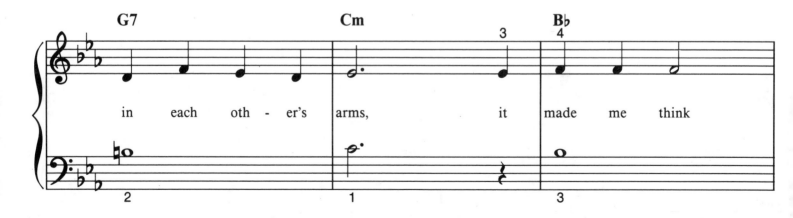

in each oth - er's arms, it made me think

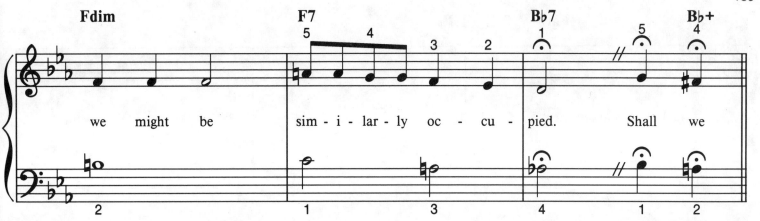

we might be sim - i - lar - ly oc - cu - pied. Shall we

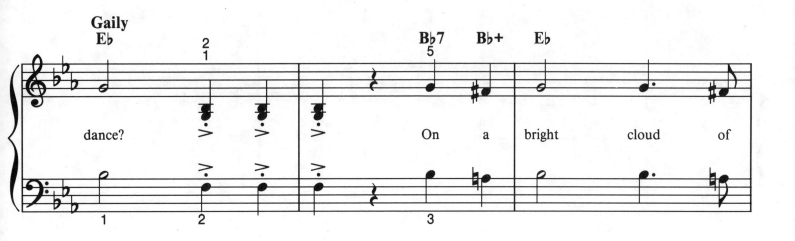

dance? On a bright cloud of

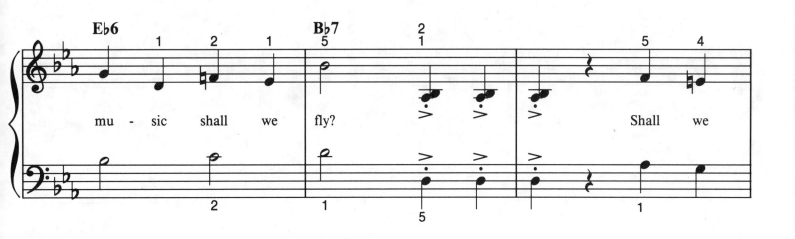

mu - sic shall we fly? Shall we

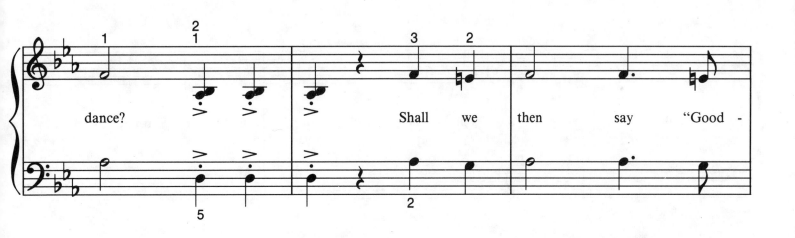

dance? Shall we then say "Good -

night" and mean "Good - bye?" Or, per -

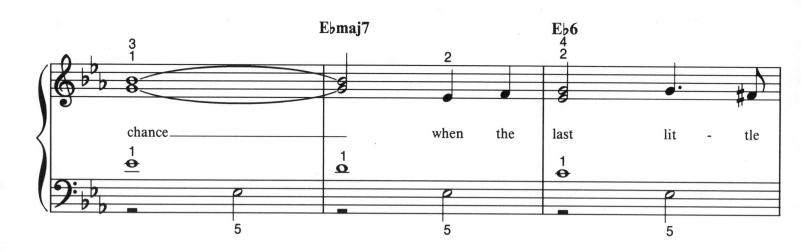

chance_____ when the last lit - tle

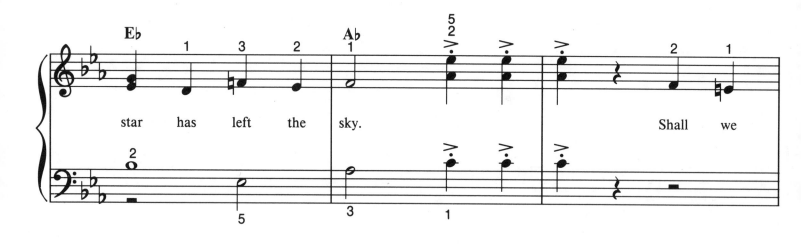

star has left the sky. Shall we

still be to - geth - er with our arms a - round each

141

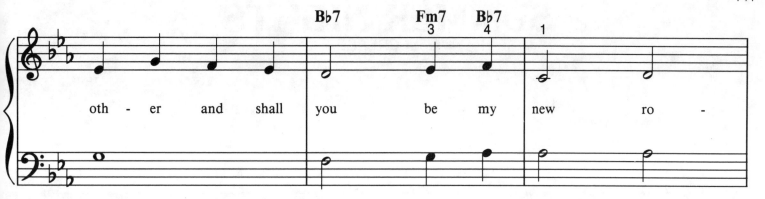

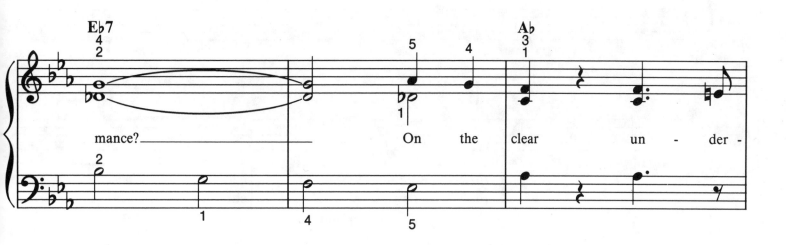

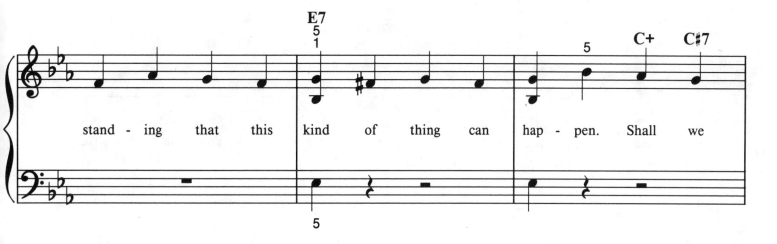

SUMMER NIGHTS

from GREASE

Lyric and Music by WARREN CASEY
and JIM JACOBS

Bb　　　　**Eb**　　**Ab**　　**F**　　**Bb**

nights.　　*Boys:* Tell me more,　tell　me　more,　like you don't have to

Eb　　**Ab**　　**F**　　**Bb7**　　**Eb**　**Ab**　**Bb**　**Ab**

brag. *Girls:* Tell me more, tell me　more, 'cause he sounds like a　drag.

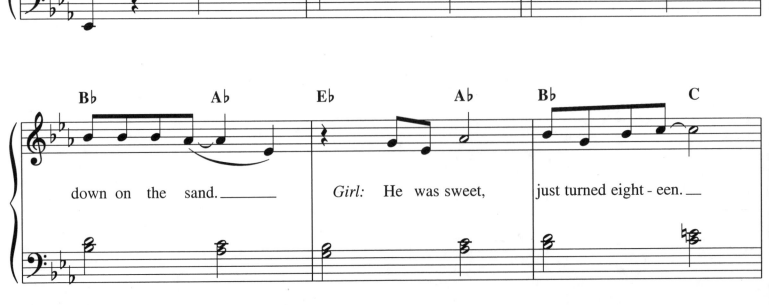

Eb　　**Ab**　　**Bb**　　**Ab**　　**Eb**　　**Ab**

Girl: He　got friend-ly　　hold-ing my　hand. _　　*Boy:* She　got friend-ly

Bb　　**Ab**　　**Eb**　　**Ab**　　**Bb**　　**C**

down　on　the　sand.＿＿＿　　*Girl:* He　was sweet,　just turned eight - een. _

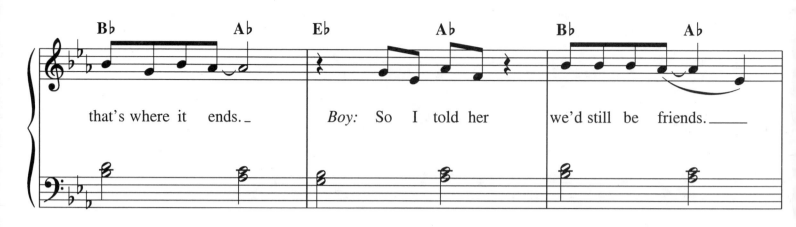

that's where it ends._ *Boy:* So I told her we'd still be friends._____

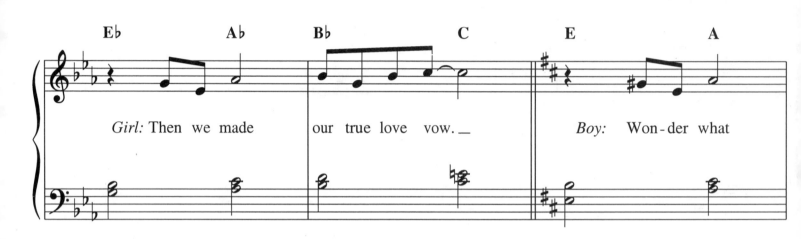

Girl: Then we made our true love vow._ *Boy:* Won-der what

Lightly

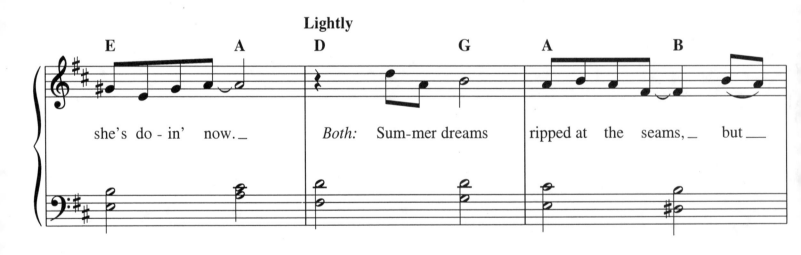

she's do-in' now._ *Both:* Sum-mer dreams ripped at the seams,_ but__

oh, those sum-mer nights._ *Chorus:* Tell me more, tell me more.

SUN AND MOON
from MISS SAIGON

Music by CLAUDE-MICHEL SCHÖNBERG
Lyrics by RICHARD MALTBY Jr. and ALAIN BOUBLIL
Adapted from original French Lyrics by ALAIN BOUBLIL

You are ___ sun - light ___ and I moon, ___

joined by ___ the gods of for - tune, ___ mid - night ___ and

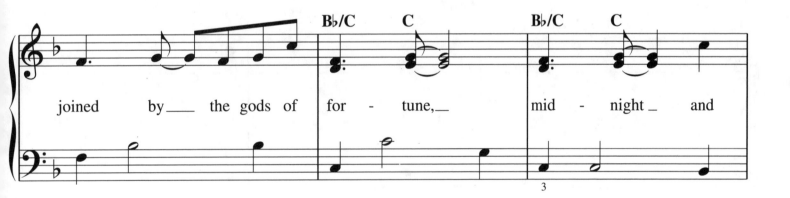

high noon ___ shar - ing ___ the sky.

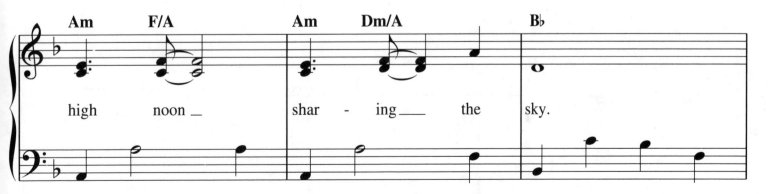

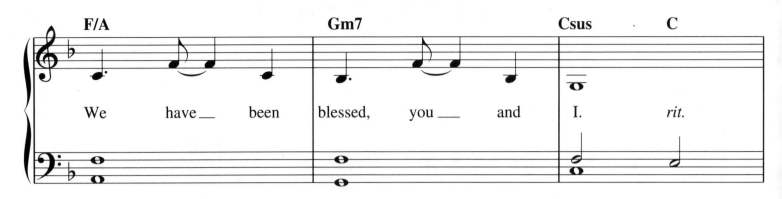

We have ___ been blessed, you ___ and I. *rit.*

CHRIS:

a tempo

You are ___ here like ___ a mys - t'ry. ___

I'm from ___ a world that's ___ so dif - f'rent ___ from

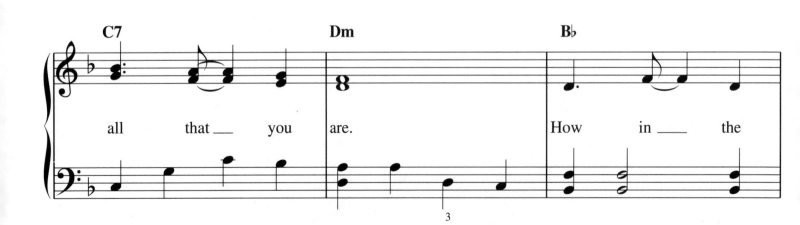

all that ___ you are. How in ___ the

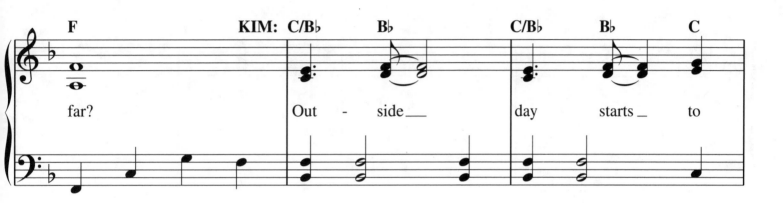

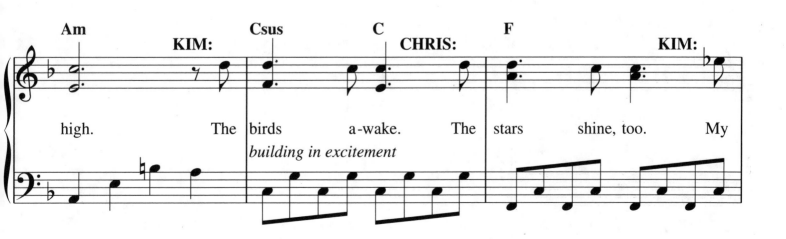

B♭7sus   **B♭7**   CHRIS: **B♭7sus**   **B♭7**   BOTH: **B♭**   **B♭7**

hands   still shake.   I   reach   for you,   and we meet in the

E♭   **A♭/E♭**

sky.
ff

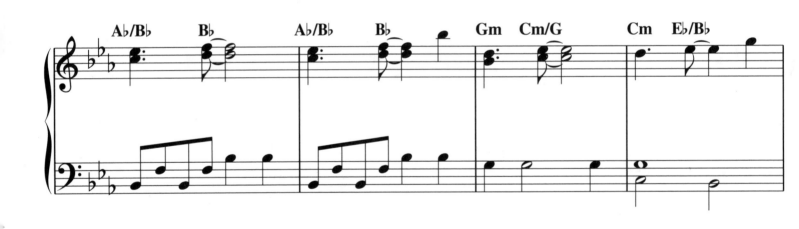

A♭/B♭   **B♭**   **A♭/B♭**   **B♭**   **Gm**   **Cm/G**   **Cm**   **E♭/B♭**

A♭   **E♭/G**   **Fm7**   **B♭7**

rit.

151

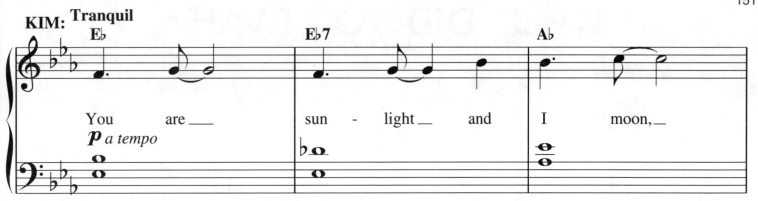

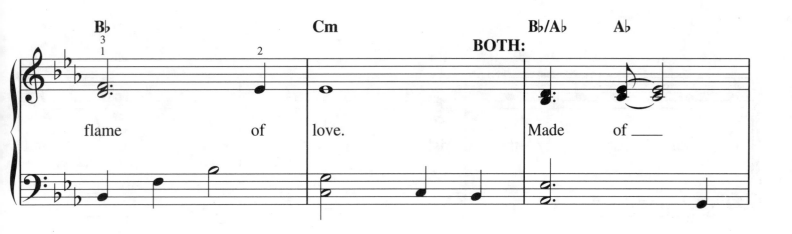

WELL, DID YOU EVAH?
from HIGH SOCIETY

Words and Music by
COLE PORTER

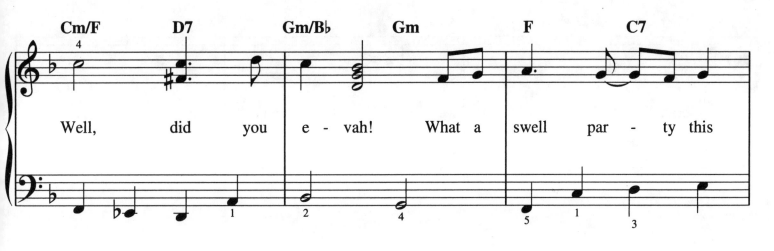

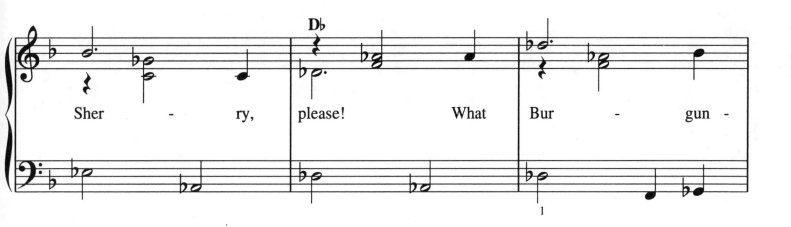

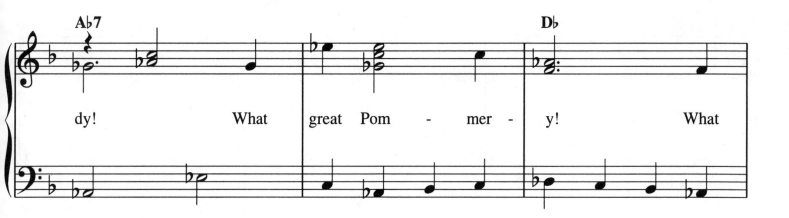

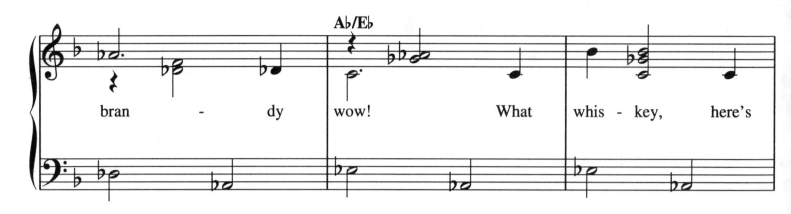

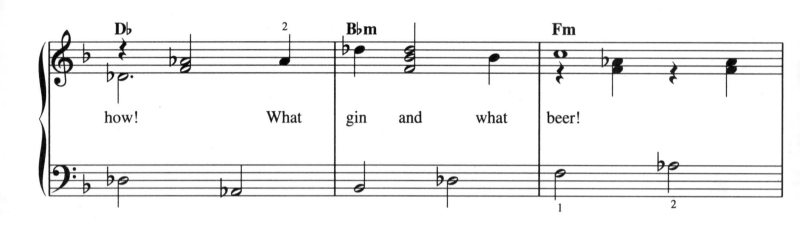

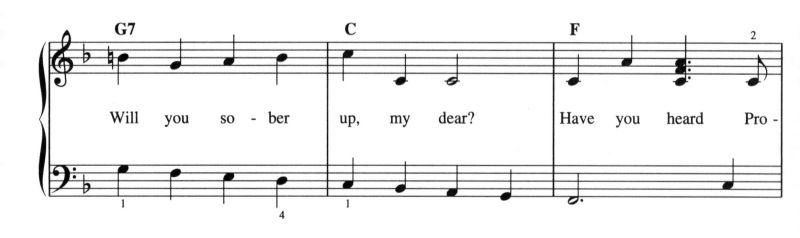

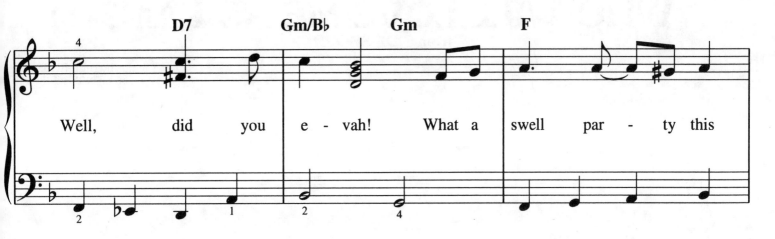

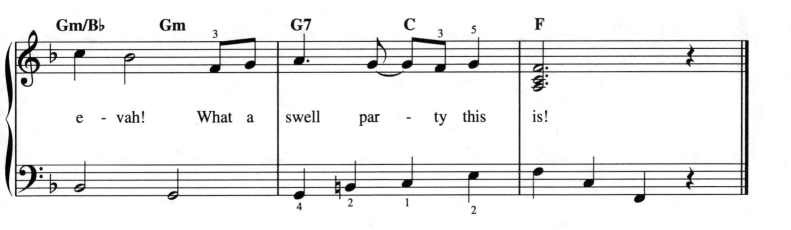

WHO WILL LOVE ME AS I AM?

from SIDE SHOW

Words by BILL RUSSELL
Music by HENRY KRIEGER

Ballad

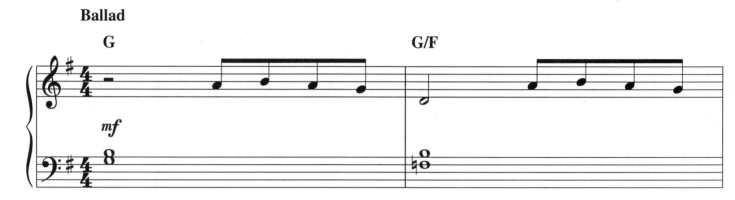

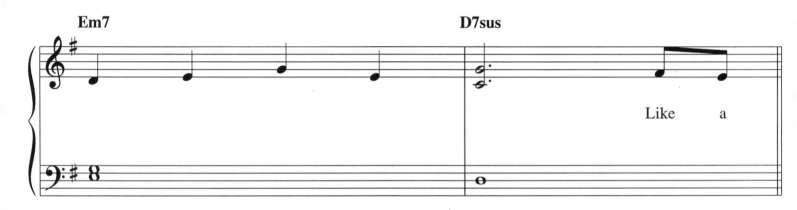

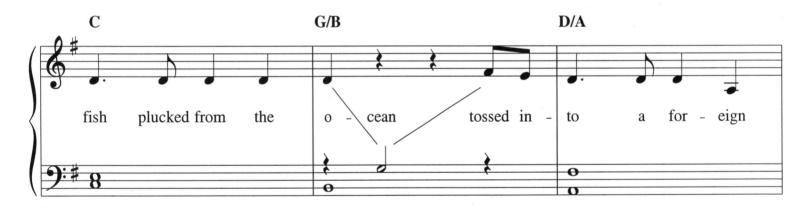

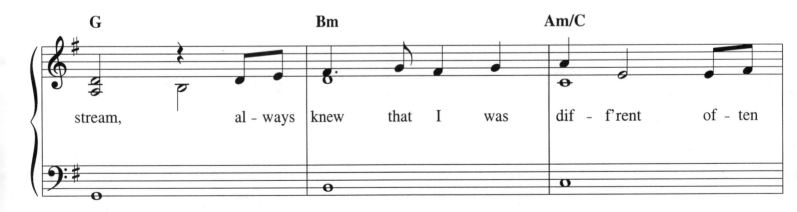

fled in - to a dream. I ig - nored the rag - ing

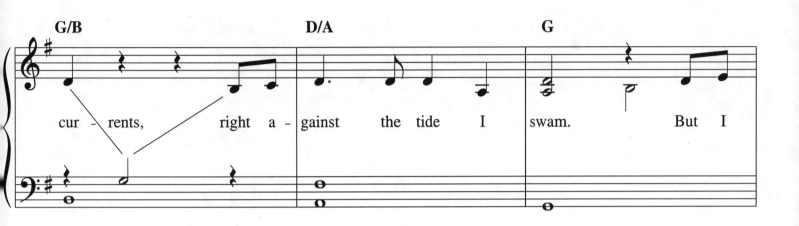

cur - rents, right a - gainst the tide I swam. But I

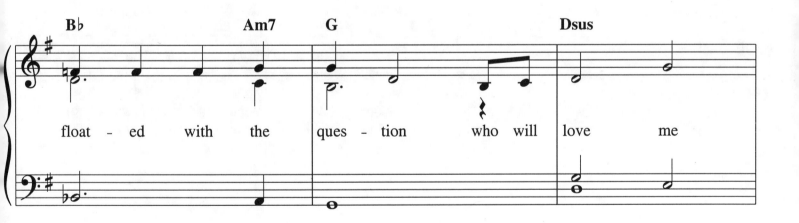

float - ed with the ques - tion who will love me

as I am? Like an

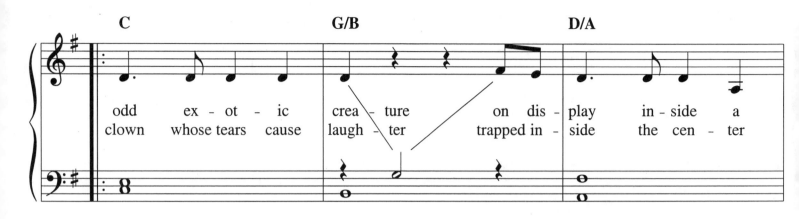

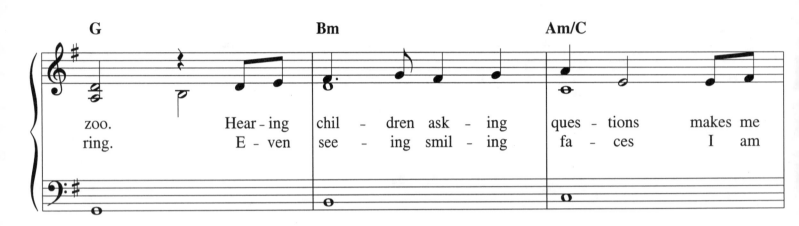

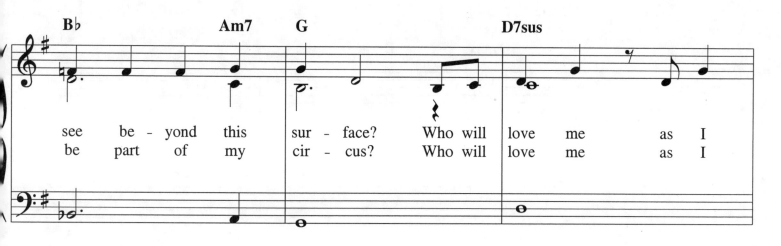
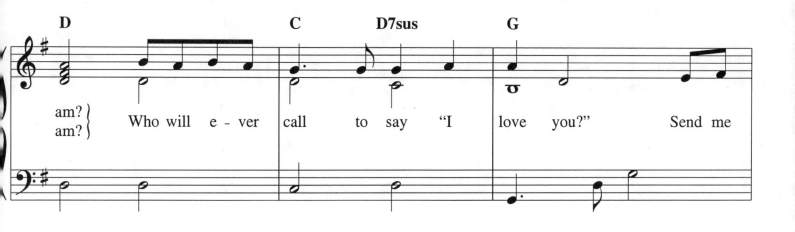
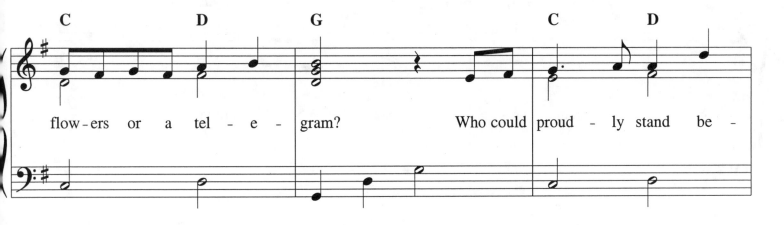

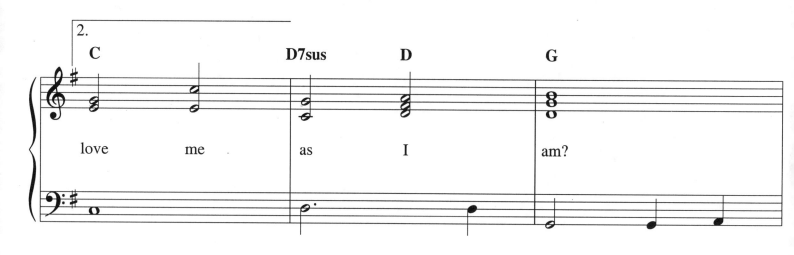

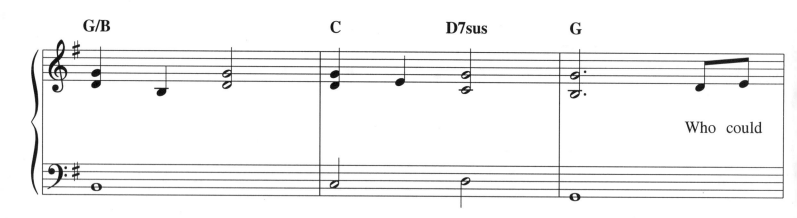

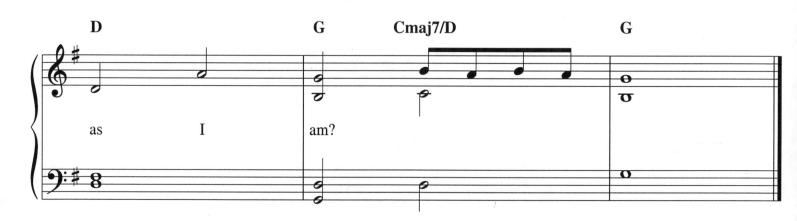

WILLKOMMEN
from the Musical CABARET

Words by FRED EBB
Music by JOHN KANDER

Gluck - lich zu se - hen Je suis en - chan - té.
Wie gehts? *Commen sa va?* *Do you feel good?*

Hap - py to see you
Ich bin euer confrencier *je siu's votre compere,*

Blei - be, Res - te, stay. Will - kom - men!
I am your host! *(Sung) Und sa - ge*

Bien - ve - nue! Wel - kome! Im Cab - a -

WITH ONE LOOK
from SUNSET BOULEVARD

Music by ANDREW LLOYD WEBBER
Lyrics by DON BLACK and CHRISTOPHER HAMPTON,
with contributions by AMY POWERS

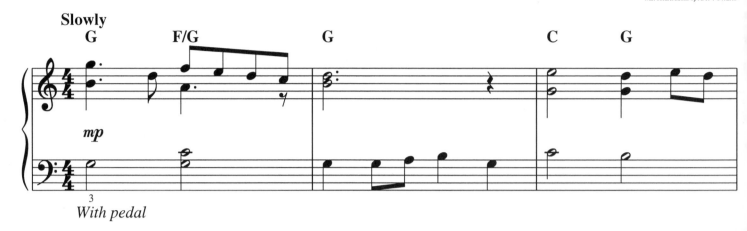

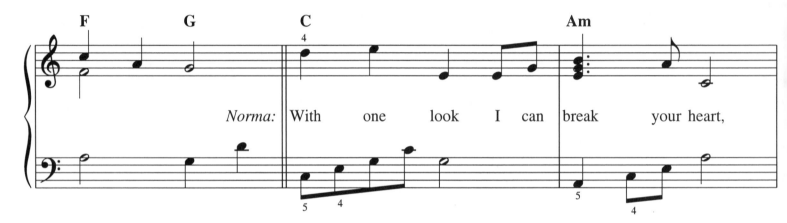

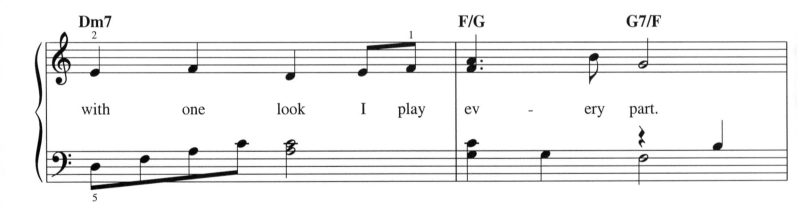

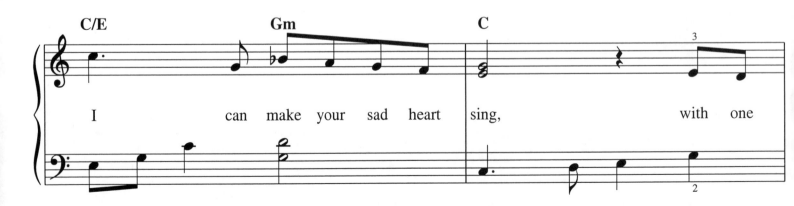

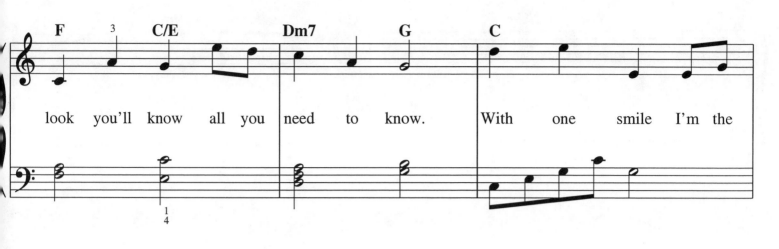

look you'll know all you need to know. With one smile I'm the

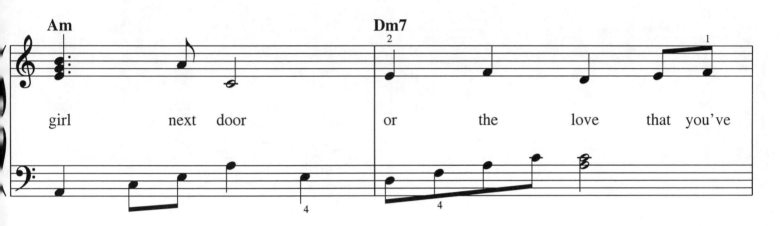

girl next door or the love that you've

hun - gered for. When I speak it's with my

soul I can play an - y role. No

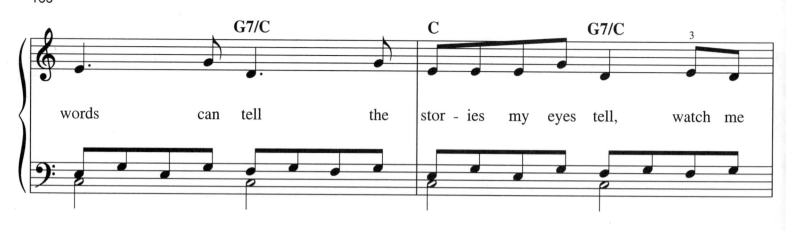

words can tell the stor- ies my eyes tell, watch me

when I frown, you can't write that down. You

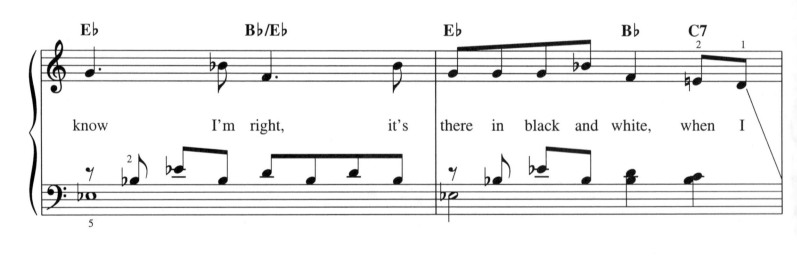

know I'm right, it's there in black and white, when I

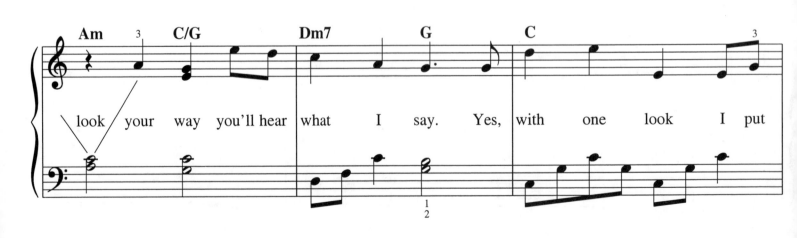

look your way you'll hear what I say. Yes, with one look I put

dark,   still   out there   in the   dark.

Si -   lent mu - sic starts   to   play.   With one

look you'll know   all you   need   to   know.   With   one   look   I'll ig -

WITHOUT YOU

from RENT

Words and Music by
JONATHAN LARSON

Moderately flowing

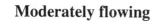
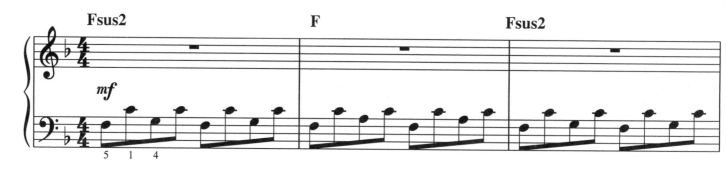

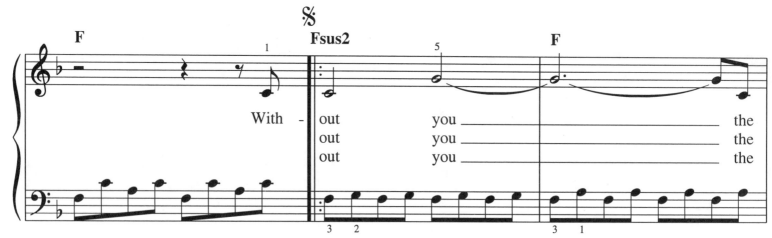

With- | out you _____ | you _____ | the
out | you _____ | the
out | you _____ | the

ground | thaws, _____ | the | rain | falls, _____
breeze | warms, _____ | the | girl | smiles, _____
hand | gropes, _____ | the | ear | hears, _____

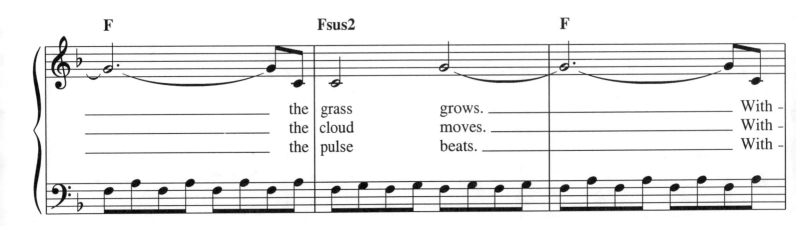

_____ | the | grass | grows. _____ | With -
_____ | the | cloud | moves. _____ | With -
_____ | the | pulse | beats. _____ | With -

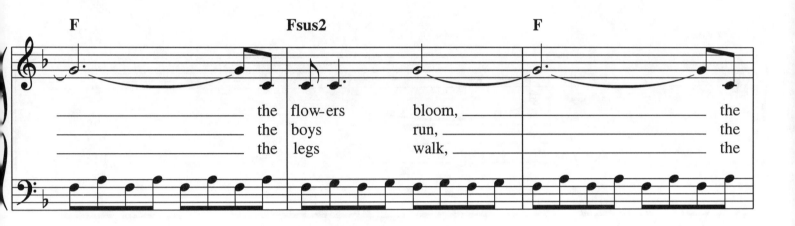

172

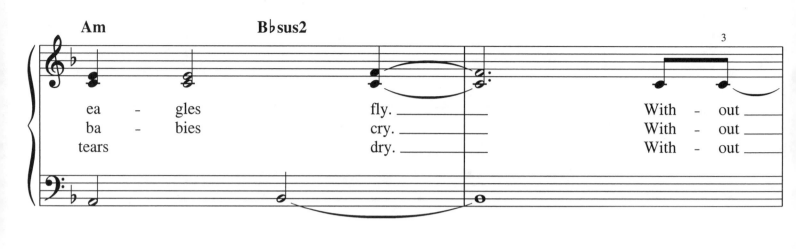

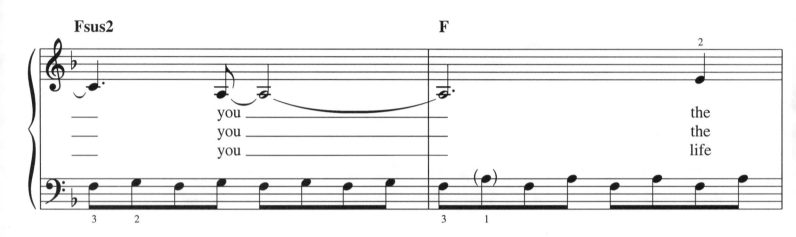

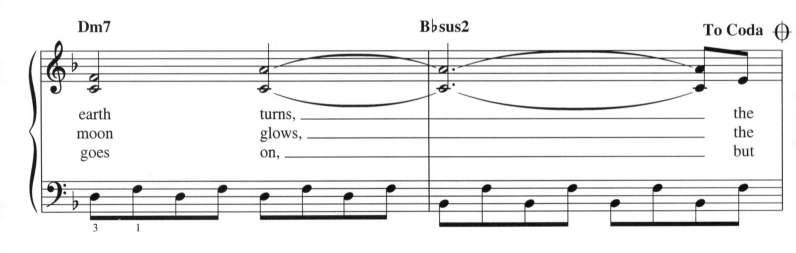

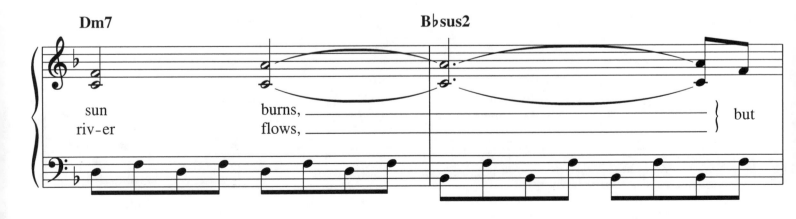

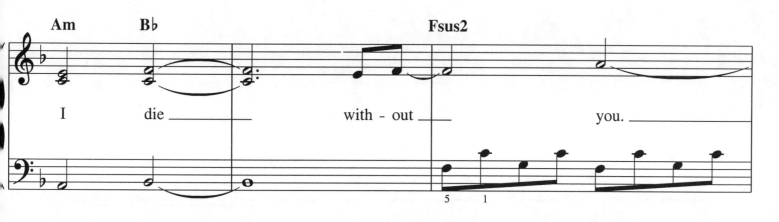

I die _____ with - out _____ you. _____

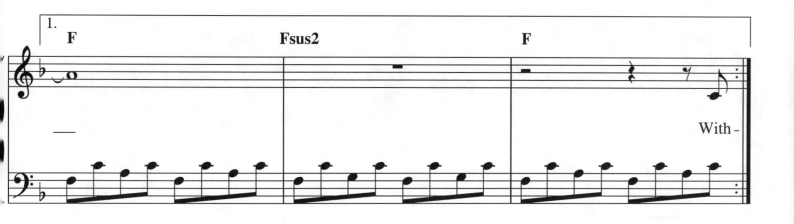

1.

_____ With -

2.

_____ The world re - vives, _____

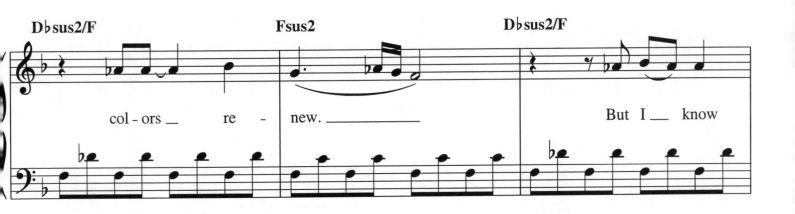

col - ors _ re - new. _____ But I _ know

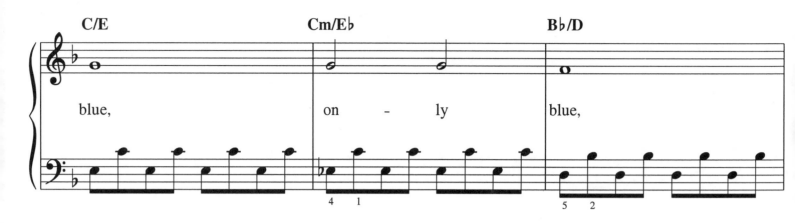

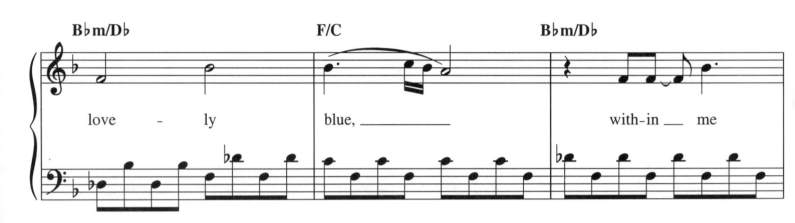

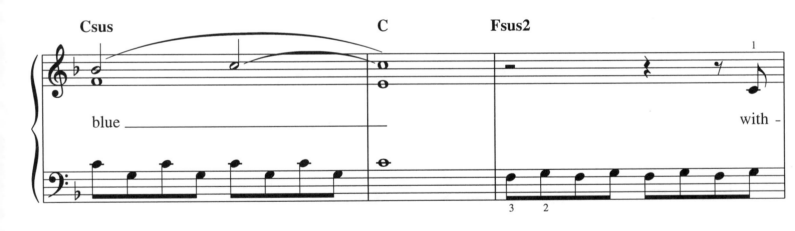

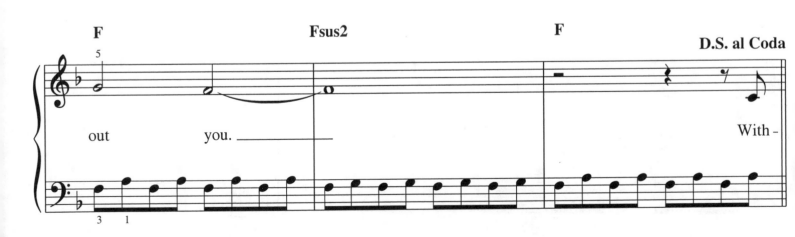

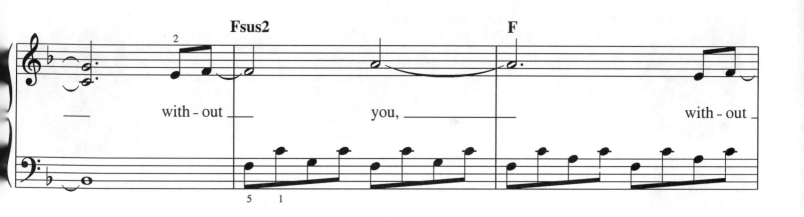

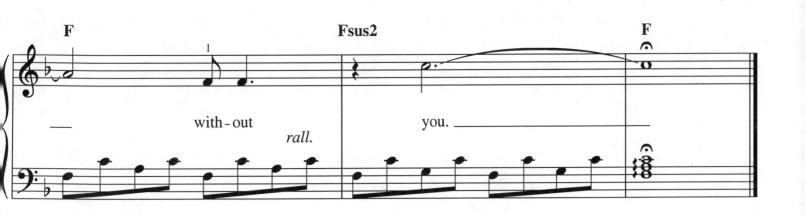

It's Easy to Play Your Favorite Songs with Hal Leonard Easy Piano Books

The Best of Today's Movie Hits
16 contemporary film favorites: Change the World • Colors of the Wind • I Believe in You and Me • I Finally Found Someone • If I Had Words • Mission: Impossible Theme • When I Fall in Love • You Must Love Me • more.
00310248 ....$9.95

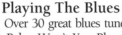

Playing The Blues
Over 30 great blues tunes arranged for easy piano: Baby, Won't You Please Come Home • Chicago Blues • Fine and Mellow • Heartbreak Hotel • Pinetop's Blues • St. Louis Blues • The Thrill Is Gone • more.
00310102...$12.95

The Best Songs Ever - 4th Edition
74 all-time favorite songs, featuring: All I Ask of You • Body and Soul • Call Me Irresponsible • Crazy • Edelweiss • Fly Me to the Moon • The Girl From Ipanema • Here's That Rainy Day • Imagine • Let It Be • Longer • Moon River • Moonlight in Vermont • People • Satin Doll • Save the Best for Last • Somewhere Out There • Stormy Weather • Strangers in the Night • Tears in Heaven • Unchained Melody • Unforgettable • The Way We Were • What a Wonderful World • When I Fall in Love • and more
00359223 ....$19.95

Country Love Songs
34 classic and contemporary country favorites, including: The Dance • A Few Good Things Remain • Forever and Ever Amen • I Never Knew Love • Love Can Build a Bridge • Love Without End, Amen • She Believes in Me • She Is His Only Need • Where've You Been • and more.
00110030 ....$12.95

R&B Love Songs
27 songs, including: Ain't Nothing Like the Real Thing • Easy • Exhale (Shoop Shoop) • The First Time Ever I Saw Your Face • Here and Now • I'm Your Baby Tonight • My Girl • Never Can Say Goodbye • Ooo Baby Baby • Save the Best for Last • Someday • Still • and more.
00310181 ....$12.95

Rock N Roll For Easy Piano
40 rock favorites for the piano, including: All Shook Up • At the Hop • Chantilly Lace • Great Balls of Fire • Lady Madonna • The Shoop Shoop Song (It's in His Kiss) • The Twist • Wooly Bully • and more.
00222544...$12.95

I'll Be Seeing You
50 Songs Of World War II
A salute to the music and memories of WWII, including a chronology of events on the homefront, dozens of photos, and 50 radio favorites of the GIs and their families back home. Includes: Boogie Woogie Bugle Boy • Don't Sit Under the Apple Tree (With Anyone Else But Me) • I Don't Want to Walk Without You • Moonlight in Vermont • and more.
00310147..$17.95

The Really Big Book of Children's Songs
63 kids' hits: Alley Cat Song • Any Dream Will Do • Circle of Life • The Grouch Song • Hakuna Matata • I Won't Grow Up • Kum-Ba-Yah • Monster Mash • My Favorite Things • Sesame Street Theme • Winnie the Pooh • You've Got a Friend in Me • and more.
00310372...$15.95

Broadway Jazz Standards
34 super songs from the stage: All the Things You Are • Bewitched • Come Rain or Come Shine • I Could Write a Book • Just in Time • The Lady Is a Tramp • Mood Indigo • My Funny Valentine • Old Devil Moon • Satin Doll • Small World • and more.
00310428...$10.95

Best Of Cole Porter
Over 30 songs, including: Be a Clown • Begin the Beguine • Easy to Love • From This Moment On • In the Still of the Night • Night and Day • So in Love • Too Darn Hot • You Do Something to Me • You'd Be So Nice to Come Home To • and more
00311576...$14.95

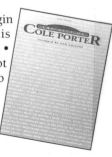

FOR MORE INFORMATION, SEE YOUR LOCAL MUSIC DEALER, OR WRITE TO:

HAL•LEONARD® CORPORATION
7777 W. BLEUMOUND RD. P.O. BOX 13819 MILWAUKEE, WI 53213

Prices, book contents, and availability subject to change without notice